DATE DUE			
FEB 10 2006			
MAR 22 2006			
DEC 08 2006			
OCT 10 2007			
FEB 04 2011			
APR 21 2011			
GAYLORD			PRINTED IN U.S.A.

WITHDRAWN FROM
CALARTS LIBRARY

ORNAMENTAL POSTERS

ORNAMENTAL POSTERS OF THE VIENNA SECESSION

WALTER KOSCHATZKY
&
HORST-HERBERT KOSSATZ

ACADEMY EDITIONS · LONDON
ST. MARTIN'S PRESS · NEW YORK

The posters in this book were first published in Publication VII of the Albertina, edited by Walter Koschatzky. They were collected in a portfolio of 34, mostly in colour, reproduced from the originals in the Albertina. Unfortunately they have to be reduced for publication from their original size, which in some cases reaches 200 × 80 cm.

CALIFORNIA INSTITUTE
OF THE ARTS LIBRARY

First published in Great Britain in 1974 by
Academy Editions 7 Holland Street London W8

SBN 85670 117 3

Copyright © Residenz Verlag 1970. All rights reserved

English translation copyright © Academy Editions 1974

First published in the U.S.A. in 1974 by St. Martin's Press Inc.
175 Fifth Avenue New York N.Y. 10010

Library of Congress Catalog Card Number 74-78171

Printed and bound in Great Britain by
Burgess & Son (Abingdon) Ltd Abingdon Oxfordshire

CONTENTS

Acknowledgements — 6

List of Colour Plates — 7

List of Black and White Illustrations — 7

Introduction *by* Walter Koschatzky — 9

The World of Poster Art — 11

Ornament and Pattern — 15

The Viennese *Jugendstil* — 21

The Posters — 29

The Plates — 35

Poster Printing Techniques — 107

Chronological table of events in the Vienna art world at the turn of the century — 112

The Artists — 115

Poster Exhibitions — 117

Bibliography — 118

Periodicals — 119

Exhibition Catalogues — 119

ACKNOWLEDGEMENTS

The editor and the author wish to thank Frau Kristin Widlar for her dedicated co-operation, and Frau Dr Judith Koós and Herr Dr Karel Holešovsky for their invaluable suggestions. We must also thank the following who have generously allowed us to reproduce copyrighted works: Professor Remigius Geyling, Frau Imelda Andri (Ferdinand Andri), Frau Lydia Hecher (Berthold Löffler), Frau Karla Hoffmann (Josef Hoffmann), Frau Marianne Klostermann (Joseph Maria Olbrich), Frau Magdalene Saiko (Rudolf Junk), Herr Dr Wolfgang Fischer (Oskar Kokoschka), Herr Karl Moser (Koloman Moser), Herr Dr Peter Pirchan (Emil Pirchan), Herr Julius Zimpel (Gustav Klimt). Despite careful endeavour we have been unable to locate the whereabouts of the remaining artists. To the detriment of the book, we have regretfully had to forego publishing the posters designed by Alfred Roller for the fourteenth and sixteenth exhibitions of the *Secession*, because the Albertina was unable to obtain permission from the copyright holders for us to reproduce them.

Walter Koschatsky
Horst-Herbert Kossatz

THE COLOUR PLATES	EMIL PIRCHAN	Emil Pirchan, Stage Designs [1913]
	HEINRICH LEFLER	Auer light [1895]
	KOLOMAN MOSER	Fromme's Calendar [1899]
	GUSTAV KLIMT	First Exhibition of the *Secession* [1898]
	BERTHOLD LÖFFLER	Arts Review, Vienna 1908 [1908]
	VIKTOR SCHUFINSKY	Lucifer [c. 1904]
	IMRE SIMAY	Nineteenth Exhibition of the *Hagenbund* [1906]
	JULIUS KLINGER	Gramophone [c. 1902]
	OSKAR KOKOSCHKA	Arts Review, Vienna 1908 [1908]
	KOLOMAN MOSER	Fifth Exhibition of the *Secession* [1899]
	JULIUS KLINGER	Spring Show [1914]
	JOSEF MARIA AUCHENTALLER	Postcard Lottery [1900]
THE BLACK AND WHITE ILLUSTRATIONS	HANS SCHLIESSMAN	Jacobi Antinicotin [1890]
	ARNOŠT HOFBAUER	Topićův salon [1898]
	JOSEPH MARIA OLBRICH	Second Exhibition of the *Secession* [1898]
	ERNST DEUTSCH	Salamander [1912]
	ADOLF KARPELLUS	Julius Meinl's Malt Coffee [1899]
	ANONYMOUS (MONOGRAMME A.K.)	Tobacco Authority [c. 1900]
	JOSEF HOFFMANN	Vienna Workshop (blue) [1905]
	FRANTIŠEK KYSELA	Svedske Umeni [1911]
	ERWIN PUCHINGER and FERDINAND PAMBERGER	Advertising Ball [1900]

THE BLACK AND WHITE ILLUSTRATIONS

KOLOMAN MOSER	Thirteenth Exhibition of the *Secession* [1902]
LEOPOLD BURGER	*The Fateful Crown* [1902]
LEOPOLD FORSTNER	Vienna Art in the Home [1903?]
JULIUS KLINGER	Third International Motor Exhibition [1903]
JOSEF HOFFMANN	Vienna Workshop (red) [1905]
LEOPOLD STOLBA	Twenty-third Exhibition of the *Secession* [1905]
FERDINAND ANDRI	Twenty-sixth Exhibition of the *Secession* [1906]
REMIGIUS GEYLING	Colosseum: Princess X [c. 1908]
LEOPOLD FORSTNER	The Modern Office [1909]
J. BERAN	Etrich Monoplane [1911]
ERWIN PUCHINGER	Vienna Union of Arts and Crafts [1912]
RUDOLF JUNK	Extraordinary State Lottery [1913]
MICHAEL BIRO	Allatkert [1914]

I Shredded banana leaves: Plate from Friedrich Deneken, *Japanische Motive für Flächenverzierung, Ein Formenschatz für das Kunstgewerbe*

II Egyptian ornamental patterns: Plate from Owen Jones, *The Grammar of Ornament*

III Japanese enamel ornaments: Plate from M. A. Racinet, *L'Ornement polychrome*

IV Tree of typical pattern shapes, units and systems: Plate from Walter Crane, *Line and Form*

V Lithographic direct flat-bed machine at the turn of the century

INTRODUCTION
by
Walter Koschatzky

Far too little research has been published—or even undertaken—on the poster collection of the Albertina Museum in Vienna. When, therefore, thanks to a scholarship from the Fritz Thyssen Institute, an opportunity arose for Horst-Herbert Kossatz to make a study of the posters, the Albertina gladly took advantage of this so that some of them might be published in large format, in a manner worthy of the museum's tradition of facsimile.

For centuries men had spoken of pure art as opposed to functional art, so that many spheres of artistic activity, including the art of the poster, were dismissed as of little value. Today, however, hardly any field of art arouses such general interest as these graphic examples of street art.

It is all the more strange that the Viennese poster art should have remained unknown until today. Whereas in England and France art dealers were already endeavouring to satisfy collectors as early as the turn of the century, in Vienna the whole of the poster production was used in advertising, which accounts for the rarity of early examples. In addition it was actually forbidden in Vienna to sell posters to private persons whose interest in them was purely artistic. It is fortunate then, that in spite of this there existed in Vienna a collector who worked under great difficulties but also with great flair and persistence; his collection formed the main basis of the Albertina's poster collection.

Dr. Ottokar Mascha, who was born in Pilsen in 1852 and became a lawyer in Prague, arrived in Vienna in 1897. Having acquired a fortune, he was able to devote himself to his interests in books and art. He owned some paintings of considerable artistic value, but was interested above all in the collection of graphic art, his tastes ranging from drawing to the long-neglected art of reproduction. Mascha succeeded, by purchasing the Viennese Wolter collection and the Griesbach collection from Berlin, in uniting practically the entire graphic output of Felicien Rops, so that in the end he possessed about 1200 drawings, etchings, lithographs, and 70 books illustrated by Rops, a collection which was purchased *en bloc* by the Belgian Government in 1921. But it was in the field of poster art that Ottokar Mascha established himself as a patron. At an early date he handed over 400 posters to the Imperial Institute of Graphic Arts, gathered mainly for teaching purposes. Important historical examples from his collection were shown in the *Secession* exhibition of 1912, for which he wrote the introduction to the catalogue. In 1913 he owned about 2500 posters, later roughly twice that number; in 1917 he presented three-quarters of his collection to the Department of Prints and Drawings of the Imperial Library, which was to be amalgamated two years later with the Albertina. Until his death in Vienna in 1929, Ottokar Mascha's time was occupied in encouraging poster art; as far back as 1913 he had founded a club for its devotees. And it is certainly due to his efforts that we owe the extraordinary blossoming of Austrian poster art in the twenties. The Mascha collection in the Albertina today comprises some 3100 posters, of which about 1360 come from the former Austro-Hungarian Empire, 720 from Germany and 430 from France.

The second half of the Albertina poster collection can be traced back to that Julius Paul who is mentioned in the list of collecting members of the poster club as owning 2500 posters; these were acquired through the firm of Nebenhay on 1 June 1939. This part of the collection, together with new acquisitions, today numbers some 6300 pieces.

1873, the year of the World Exhibition, marks a turning point for Vienna. Hardly any field of activity remained untouched by it. There was a mood of change, inspired by the unattainable desire to amalgamate rival cultures into one world culture. We must remember here the influence of Japan on European art. This began in the mid-nineteenth century, after Trade Treaties with the U.S.A., England, France and Russia had opened contacts with Japan. Japanese woodcuts were shown at the World Exhibition in London in 1862, in Paris in 1867, in 1873 in Vienna, and in 1878 once more in Paris, where Japanese exhibits proved the main attraction. This influence has never really been studied, but its connection with Art Nouveau and with poster art is undeniably important. Günther Busch was quite correct in stating (in the catalogue of the Exhibition of European Art Nouveau, Bremen, 1965) that the Art Nouveau Revolution had taken place on paper, mainly as the fantasies of architects and as graphic art. This can be further expanded by stating that in graphic art it was mainly poster art which epitomized the style of the period. The elements which Christian von Heusinger judged as essentially Japanese were the ornamental ordering of surfaces, the calligraphy of Japanese line-drawing, the silhouette form of the figures, the bold outline of the picture and the exaggeration of the main focal points of interest. Each of these elements has also become part of the technique of poster art, the most important obviously being the ornamentation. Pierre Bonnard was once asked what he had taken over from Japanese art. His reply was: 'The lovely patterns'!

This work seeks to show the development of ornamental art at the turn of the century from the traditions of historicism. Thus when the Albertina publishes a group of ornamental posters from Vienna designed around 1900, it is not merely an exhibition of material, but also a contribution to a total picture of Viennese art between 1890 and 1914.

Walter Koschatzky.

THE WORLD OF POSTER ART

Good posters influence the viewer in spite of himself. They do not have to be liked by the individual, but they must be noticed by all. It may be debated, and frequently has been, whether a poster should display more or fewer words, whether the message should strike the viewer like a flash of lightning or subtly influence his subconscious. But there can be no doubt that the effectiveness of a poster increases, the more unconventional and startling it is.

The creation of artistic posters—and these are the only ones discussed here—is one of the few fields of art today where the old relationship of customer and artist is preserved, albeit in a new form. The artist must be guided by the wishes of the customer, he must fulfil an advertising contract, and his success is judged not solely by artistic standards, but chiefly by the increased income of the customer. It is, therefore, a happy chance when a poster retains its effect and survives its (usually inartistic) purpose of advertisement; and yet this is at the same time a contradiction, since the advertising poster, created in order to sell goods and to notify the public of events and decrees, should really be obsolete when it has fulfilled this purpose. Nevertheless, when it has fulfilled its original purpose, it is able to influence later ages as a historical document and a reflection of its time, and also as a work of art.

Like a drummer who attracts attention through sound, poster advertising works on our senses by means of optical effects to capture our attention and strengthen our interest in amusements or industrial products. In the course of its development, advertising through calling, shouting or enticing has developed into the present day advertising, which uses subtle persuasion and seeks to awaken in the viewer the desire to buy.

In the early nineteenth century, posters consisted solely of texts. Many were forbidden on political grounds, so those who affixed them had to develop special methods of illegal advertising. An instance is cited of a man with a large basket on his back coming along the street. He peers round to make sure he is unobserved, and then he leans towards the wall with the basket, out of which a small boy emerges and sticks up the text. Since some houses, especially in London, were soon completely covered by such advertisements, a remedy was found. Licensed advertising hoardings were set up, where space could be rented, or advertising pillars on wheels, illuminated from within, drove continuously around the town day and night. In this way, advertising became a daily occurrence, as the town criers had been. These advertising machines, which were in use around 1825 in London and Paris, did not last, although they were established well in advance of the Litfass pillars set up in Berlin in 1885 by Ernst Litfass.

This permanent 'street exhibition' soon extended to the premises of the World Exhibition, the domain of the industrial arts. With a complete absence of proper respect a number of crafts had joined the fine arts—the product of a new field of human intelligence, now known as technology. In 1837 Karl Karmarsch, the most important technologist of the nineteenth century, wrote that technology 'has as its object the systematic description of those processes and tools by which Nature's raw materials are manufactured into objects of everyday use. It therefore excludes all branches which seek solely to satisfy a sense of beauty or some other intellectual sense (e.g. painting, pure sculpture etc.)'

Technological expertise also influenced applied art, and Gottfried Semper spoke of the 'technical arts'. With the adaptation of art to technology—the reverse has never occurred—new concepts were invented: 'arts and crafts' and 'the industrial arts'. Such coining of words showed the tremendous confusion in art terminology at that time, when mechanical production was set up as an ideal, in opposition to traditional craft. The definition of 'industry' found in old dictionaries—'diligence in craftsmanship'—was characteristic of these industrial arts, which frequently valued the artefact above the work of art. For these reasons it is not surprising that it was then that those artistically worthless chromolithographic posters became popular. They were, it is true, produced from twenty or thirty different colour plates, but because of the many layers of colour ended up in varying shades of brown with a speckled glaze caused by too much binder.
In printing, too, technology played a vitally important role, owing to the great interest in the mechanics of duplicating, the new planographic printing and the advances made in the construction of direct flat-bed machines. The picture poster was to be—together with the many illustrated newspapers—the main product of this development.

It required all the numerous inventions of a century passionately interested in printing to make possible the picture poster. The invention of lithography by Aloys Senefelder in 1796 was not sufficient. At that time the vats could only produce paper of comparatively small format, much too small for posters. But in 1799 Louis Robert had already succeeded in constructing an efficient paper-machine which could produce paper of any length, and this invention soon made it possible to replace the expensive rags to some extent by cheap filler. With the invention of machine paper a new era of teaching and knowledge, of information and communication, began—an era based on the global dissemination of word and picture. Only machine paper made possible the invention by Friedrich König in 1811 of the letterpress printing machine, which was to be so important for continuous newspaper-printing.
Machine paper became the material basis of the large-scale poster intended to be effective at a distance. The invention of the letterpress printing machine tormented the lithographers, who were still obliged to print each page by hand, and colour by colour. In 1832 the brothers Heim were already building English high-speed printing machines in Offenbach and exporting them to many countries. It was at this time too that lithographic printing, so important for the printing of coloured posters, was invented, although it was seen first as a method of reproducing lithographic prints of oil paintings, a process which has long since vanished. It is true that Charles Louis Malapeau had taken out a patent on his process for the lithographic printing of oil paintings—nevertheless the Société d'Encouragement, which so ably encouraged industrial progress, established in 1828 a prize for this branch of printing, which was not awarded until 1838, when it was presented to Gottfried Engelmann.
Austria also played her part in the development of lithography. At the Third Austrian General Trades Fair in 1845, Gustav Pfannkuche, the Viennese machine manufacturer and pin-factory owner, exhibited a high-speed lithographic printing machine. Soon, the high-speed

cylinder printing machine which Georg Sigl had built in 1854 in the Vienna machine factory for the State Printers became known all over Europe. The whole process was practically completed by the World Exhibition of 1867 in Paris, where many high-speed lithographic printing machines of all kinds were exhibited. Here, too, for the first time lithographic machines for printing on metal plates were displayed, the forerunners of the offset principle. In the Vienna World Exhibition of 1873, metal posters printed by such machines covered whole wall surfaces in the agricultural hall. These metal posters, apparently so durable, have long since vanished from the walls. No-one collected them; the collectors had enough to do looking after and storing paper posters.

The development of an artistic poster style is due in great measure to Jules Chéret, who personally drew his designs on the stone. At that time a poster had to be so dramatic that it would make a spontaneous impression on the beholder. In order to achieve this dramatic quality, the poster had to be sensational, but this aspect should not obscure the main purpose of the poster. From the very beginning lascivious representations of Woman were chosen to arouse this sensation, and when Chéret adopted this for the first time in 1896 the artistic picture poster was born. Chéret, who produced over one thousand designs, was able to blend in nuances from Japanese courtesans on the one hand and on the other from English and French drawings, particularly those of Alfred Grévin, whose principal theme was the life of the Parisian *demi-mondaine*.

These grisettes, cocottes, dancers and singers remained popular, particularly in France, until the turn of the century; the *demi-mondaine* was counted an essential attribute of a good poster, although she had seldom any genuine connection with the goods being advertised. Although this *demi-monde* had been discovered by literature and the fine arts—one had only to think of the masterly descriptions of Emile Zola and of the paintings of Alexandre Cabanel, Léon Gérôme and later Toulouse-Lautrec—nevertheless, the poster, without pursuing any high ideals, also played its small part in the *fin de siècle*.

The authorities of course sought to suppress this exaggerated display of the female form. Posters which were particularly daring were forbidden or had to be partially pasted over; in England the censor's office even restricted them to the higher parts of advertisement hoardings, so that no unauthorized scribblers could embellish them. Of course, there were those who sought to reverse the immoral influence of these posters by giving a better example. A Union pour l'Action Morale decided to combat indecent posters with decent ones. They hoped for great results from the duplication as a giant poster of that enormous painting by Puvis de Chavannes in the Panthéon which portrays the youth of St. Geneviève, so that they could join with the patron saint of Paris in battle against their adversaries. Even before they appeared, the posters were widely advertised in the press, and thus half the effect was lost. And since only ten posters were set up, and these in the best quarter of Paris, their success was ephemeral.

The slogan of Ruskin and Morris—Art for the people—was fulfilled for a time by wallpaper, but otherwise only truly by poster art. This street art, although a poor man's art, also awoke the interest of collectors, in the same way as the etching, which was esteemed more highly than the text it illustrated. Publishers on the lookout for money brought out editions of the most popular posters for sale. Even before 1900 there were collections numbering 10,000 items. French collectors removed posters from the walls when they thought themselves unobserved; collectors in England bribed the bill-stickers and were in their turn blackmailed by them. There were even dealers who produced posters solely to sell to collectors, while seeming to convey a genuine advertisement. In fact they served only to enrich the dealers, and this activity was soon suppressed by the courts.

As early as 1884 the first poster exhibitions were held in Paris and Brussels. Ten years later, Joseph Weiner, the eldest son of the proprietor of the Vienna Poster Printing Works, and owner of their Paris branch, received first prize at the Exhibition du Livre for his posters. The public began to take an interest in posters. About 1895 poster exhibitions were suddenly taking place everywhere; we have documentary evidence of no fewer than thirty between 1894 and 1897 (cf. list in Appendix). In Vienna, too, a poster exhibition was held from 24 April to 1 May 1896, arranged by Carl Colbert, the director of the newspaper *Wiener Mode*.

About 1895, the first high point in poster art, so closely connected to Art Nouveau, was reached in the French and Anglo-American development. Only after 1900, influenced by Beardsley, Crane and Grasset, did an ornamental, heraldic poster style develop which relied less on flighty womanhood. It is best characterized by the remark of Julius Klinger that the best poster for the United States was the American flag.

ORNAMENT AND PATTERN

The nineteenth century loved the art of decoration; by learning to distinguish the ornamental shapes and arranging them according to styles, they thought they could understand the art of all times and all peoples; in fact they merely gained an essentially superficial knowledge of the past. This state of affairs is generally called historicism. They even thought that they understood this art of the past so well that they constructed buildings and objects using the different ornamental shapes they had discovered.

Works of art which were not decorated according to the rules of this technique of ornamentation were deemed naked and thought to require decorative ornamentation. In this connection Gottfried Semper developed his important theory of ornamentation in achitecture; Adolf Loos was the first consciously to renounce, for his house in the Michaelerplatz in Vienna, a decoration which had become simply a convention. To what extremes this *horror vacui*—the fear of empty surfaces—was to lead in the second half of the nineteenth century can be seen in a book which appeared in 1875, *Die Formensprache des Kunstgewerbes* (The language of form in arts and crafts), where it is stated that:

Those products which are completely covered with decoration are today usually called 'works of art', and correspondingly those crafts which produce such objects are called 'art crafts'. In like

I. Friedrich Deneken, *Japanische Motive für Flächenverzierung, Ein Formenschatz für das Kunstgewerbe* (Japanese motifs for surface decoration), Berlin 1897. Plate 87: Shredded banana leaves, a Japanese dyer's stencil, original size 34×37 cm.

manner the terms 'art industry' and 'technical arts' have come into current usage, indicating a similar union of artistic creation and craftsmanship.

The modes of ornamental decoration, short-lived fashions dependent on an ever-changing contemporary taste, gave rise to a new kind of industrial art; in spite of such phrases as 'industrial design', 'creation of form' or even 'styling', it frequently remained, and remains so today, the mere covering of an object with an ornamental decoration.

It is of some importance to clarify the terms used in connection with decoration. The words 'ornament' and 'pattern' are used interchangeably, although they denote different things. The word 'ornament', in its strictest sense, can only mean the motifs used in decoration, whereas 'pattern' indicates the system of decoration, i.e. the regular repetition of a decorative motif on a surface. The ornament used as a single decorative motif is emotional, confusing. The pattern as a system of decoration is regular and strictly rational. Since normally a pattern becomes visible through its decorative components the two concepts are often confused, although there is always the possibility that a pure net-like surface pattern could be produced without ornament. From what has been said it is clear that 'ornamentation', strictly speaking, is simply the storehouse of decoration.

One pattern without decoration is the chequer-board pattern, and there are other examples in heraldry. The chequer-board pattern—at one time the white squares seem to form the background, at another the black ones—is ideally qualified to demonstrate one of the structural principles of Art Nouveau. The negative background portions of the drawing were constructed at that time in such a way that they corresponded to the positive areas of the drawing, yet at the same time, in spite of the considerable variations of shape, gave the impression of a flat surface. This principle is shown very clearly by the special fondness of some famous artists of the Art Nouveau for pure black and white drawing. Of course we must mention particularly in this connection the genius Aubrey Beardsley, who died young, but we must not forget also the theorists William Morris and Walter Crane.

But the principle of this surface art really originated in Japan. Japanese art played the same sort of role in the second half of the nineteenth century that Chinese art had a century before. As early as the forced Trade Treaties and particularly after the opening of the Empire to foreigners there was a lively exchange of cultural and other wares with the West. Japanese art was introduced at the World Exhibitions, and it was described and researched in many publications. Some of these books were of a scientific character, but a large proportion were written as model and pattern books for arts and crafts. Some important examples are:

Thomas W. Cutler, *A Grammar of Japanese Ornament and Design*, 1880.

O. G. Moser, *Book of Japanese Ornament, composing Designs for the use of Signpainters, Decorators, Designers, Silversmiths, and many other purposes*, 1880.

George Ashdown Audsley, *The Ornamental Arts of Japan*, 1882.

Then from 1888 until 1891 the Hamburg art dealer and collector of things Japanese, Siegfried Bing, who was living in Paris, put out his

ORNAMENT AND PATTERN

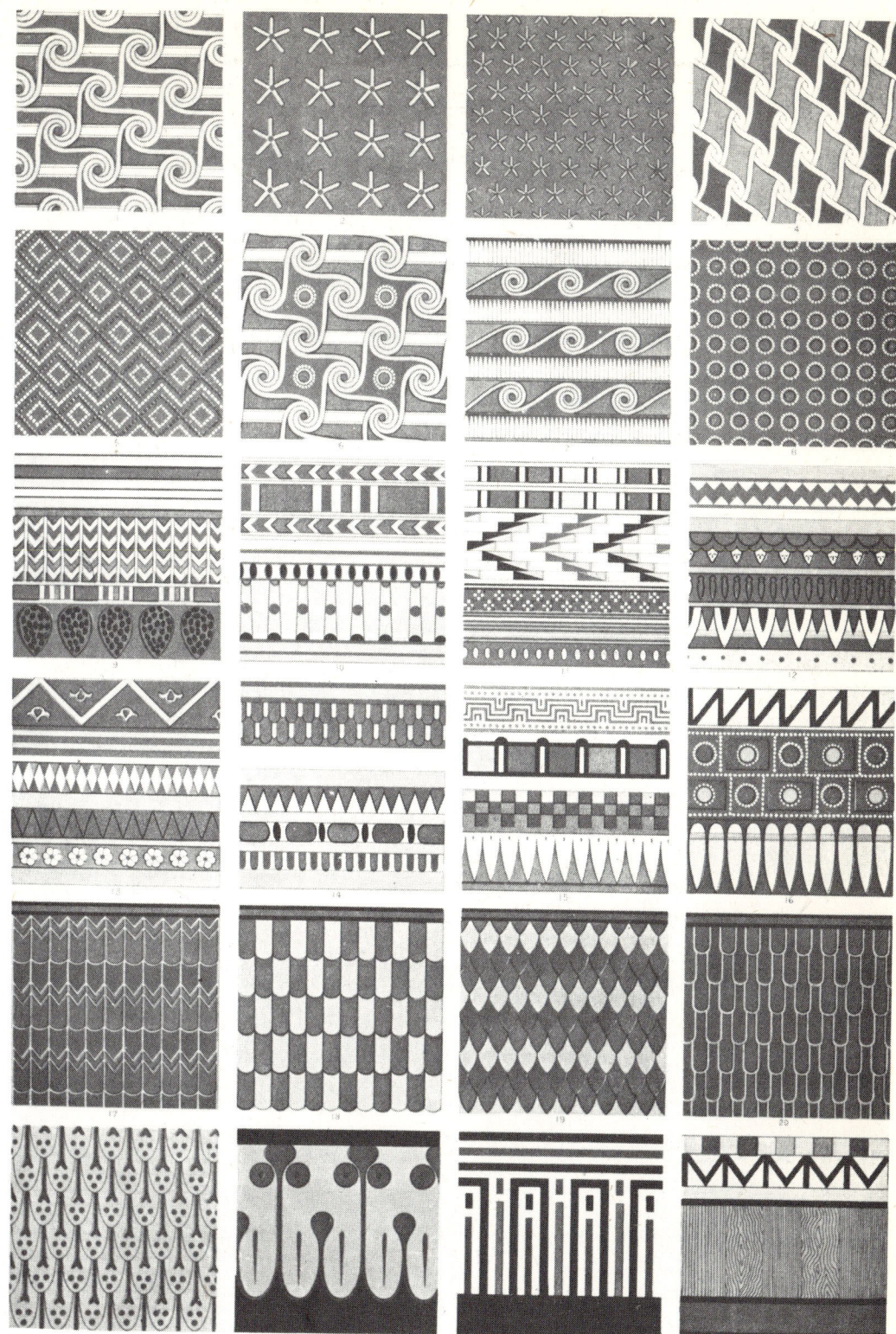

Japanischer Formenschatz (Japanese Treasury of Form), as a counterpart to Georg Hirth's famous *Treasury of Form*.

But more important than these works for the development of Art Nouveau was a series of books in which Japanese surface patterns were published. The most important are:

    J. Brinckmann, *Japanische Flächenornamente* (Japanese surface ornamentation), 1892.

    W. Tuer, *Das Buch reizender und merkwürdiger Zeichnungen* (The book of delightful and remarkable drawings), 1894.

    F. Deneken, *Japanische Motive für Flächenverzierung* (Japanese motifs for surface decoration), 1897.

The last-named book, which bears the characteristic sub-title 'A

II. Owen Jones, *The Grammar of Ornament*, London 1856. Plate XI, Egyptian ornamental patterns.

17

ORNAMENTAL POSTERS

Treasury of Form for Arts and Crafts', contained for the first time a brief historical summary of Japanism. Deneken writes:

> In conjunction with the study of the flowers of the country, the Japanese concept of Nature has penetrated particularly into one branch of arts and crafts, namely that of surface patterns. Notable artists, above all the talented painter and illustrator Walter Crane, were innovators in this respect.

And it was Crane who was to provide an important stimulus to the development of the Vienna *Jugendstil*.
The Japanese dyers' patterns, which were really intended solely for colour printing on materials and were simply a means to an end, were

III. M. A. Racinet, *L'Ornement Polychrome*, Paris 1864–1873. Plate 12, Japanese enamel ornaments.

considered at that time to be works of art on their own account and were reproduced in black and white in these books. Such patterns proved to be important sources of Japanese surface decoration. But they have another significance; for since the complicated pattern stencils were stuck on to nets, we have here a non-European forerunner of the modern silk-screen process of printing. This adoption of Japanese methods of patterning played an important part in the Vienna *Jugendstil*.

In addition to the Japanese patterns, the oriental endless pattern systems had a strong influence on Art Nouveau. As early as 1851, at the first World Exhibition, Richard Redgrave had pointed out their importance as models for mechanical motif repetition in textile weaving. Another theorist of Art Noveau, the Frenchman Eugène Grasset, based his theories on oriental ornamentation and patterns. He wrote two important works, *La Plante et ses Applications Ornamentales* (1896) and *Méthode de Composition Ornamentale* (1905). All these works—the books on Japanese ornamentation as well as those on oriental patterning—can only be understood as the second stage of historicism.

One of the characteristics of historicism was its love of patterns. A large number of copy-books was produced at that time, almost all of which are ordered according to styles. To read all of them is to gain a unique knowledge of historic ornamentation. The most important of these works are:

O. Jones, *The Grammar of Ornament*, 1856.

M. A. Racinet, *L'Ornement polychrome*, 1869–1873.

Both these books were translated into German and a number of inferior works were based on them. Not only the historicists took their motifs from them; the artists of the *Jugendstil* found inspiration here too, although they used them differently. Jones' *Grammar of Ornament* even contains plant motifs from nature on the last page.

When we study the plates of these expensive books, produced through chromolithography, we realize the the surface art of the *Jugendstil* is a result of this development. For the plates are always a composite picture of many different motifs from the one style. The blocks of colour do not, strangely enough, give an olde-worlde impression. If one adds to these pattern books the Natural History tables and systems, we have collected together the complete store of ornamental models. But all these books cause us to think of Art Nouveau, which is based on them, as a form of historicism; however, unlike the historicism generally thought of as such, this historicism did not desire to model its works of art on the past—it is to be understood rather as an aesthetic historicism, since it used the traditional ornamental motifs to build something new.

THE VIENNESE *JUGENDSTIL*

The Viennese *Jugendstil* (the German Art Nouveau movement) is a late flower. And like many such late flowers this one is particularly rich and colourful, enchanting and delicate. The movement only started with the *Secession*, unfolded after the turn of the century, and with the founding of the *Wienerwerkstätte* (Vienna Workshop) altered its image completely.

At an early date new ideas were burgeoning in the Otto Wagner circle. His school is considered to be one of the main sources in the development of modern architecture. Here we must mention, too, the Seven Club, founded in 1895. The members were the architects Josef Hoffmann, Joseph Maria Olbrich and Friedrich Pilz, and the painters Leo Kainradl, Adolf Karpellus, Max Kurzweil and Koloman Moser. Although their activity was restricted to discussion and cooperation in book illustration, their theories were to have considerable influence on further developments.

But the main impetus came from elsewhere. After disputes between the older and younger members of the *Genossenschaft bildender Kunstler Wiens* (Association of Viennese Creative Artists), known as the *Künstlerhaus*, concerning the participation of foreign artists in the exhibitions of this organization, the younger members banded together, and on 3 April 1897 their spokesman, Gustav Klimt, announced to the press and to the Committee of the *Künstlerhaus* that they had that day formed the *Vereinigung bildender Künstler Osterreichs* (Union of Creative Artists of Austria). The older generation expressed its displeasure, whereupon the younger members resigned from the Association in protest. The new *Secession* was popular with the public, and as early as 1898 they organized in the premises of the Gartenbaugesellschaft (Gardeners' Club) their first exhibition, which was a sensation in Vienna. In the introduction to the catalogue they stated:

> Since the greater part of our public has until now been left in blissful ignorance of the momentous developments in art abroad, we have tried in this, our first exhibition, to present a picture of modern art abroad, so that the public may thus obtain a new and higher standard by which to judge Austrian art.

How truly this corresponded to the needs and desires of the public can be seen from the enthusiastic words of the leading Vienna art critic of the time, Ludwig Hevesi: 'Some of the greatest living artists, completely unknown in Vienna until now, fill whole walls, even whole rooms'.

Let us, however, go back a little. The Seven Club used to meet in the rooms of the Café Sperl or in the Blaues Freihaus. For a long time previously there had been another round table of artists who called themselves the 'Hagengesellschaft' after the proprietor of the inn. From these two loosely connected clubs, together with the discontented moderns of the Artists' Association, arose that group which met in Hagen's Hotel Viktoria to prepare the ground for the planned *Secession*. This departure caused those who remained in the Blaues Freihaus to form their own union, which met as the *Hagenbund* in the *Künstlerhaus* as an independent body, and which organized two exhibitions in its own rooms. The great success which these enjoyed prompted their jealous colleagues to refuse rights to hold a third exhibition, whereupon the young union resigned from the Association in order to open its third exhibition in the Miethke Gallery. In 1902 this 'Künstlerbund Hagen' found a home in the rooms of the Zedlitzhalle which had been converted by Joseph Urban, under the presidency of his brother-in-law Heinrich Lefler. That Urban and Lefler were not accepted into the *Secession* may be due to the fact that as late as 24 March 1897 they had received the Imperial Prize of the 25th Annual Exhibition of the *Künstlerhaus*.

From the very beginning the *Secession* stressed the importance of participation in international art, hoping thus to enrich Viennese art and give it once again an important position in European art. The support of foreign artists for this aim is shown by the many entries from corresponding members. In 1898 the list already reads like an index from a history of contemporary art: Bartholomé, Besnard, Boutet de Monvel, Brangwyn, Burne-Jones, Carrière, Charpentier, Crane, Grasset, Max Klinger, Puvis de Chavannes, Rodin, Rops, Segantini, Stuck, Thoma, Uhde, Whistler and Zorn are some of the names. As early as 1898 an exhibition was held in the exhibition rooms designed by Olbrich, and in the same year, too, the first number of the *Secession* magazine had appeared, whose title *Ver Sacrum* presumably referred to Uhland's poem of the same name, which describes the Roman 'Sacred Spring', and the last verse of which runs:

> Ihr habt vernommen, was dem Gott gefällt.
> Geht hin, bereitet euch, gehorchet still!
> Ihr seid das Saatkorn einer neuen Welt,
> Das ist der Weihefrühling, den er will.
>
> (You have heard the pleasure of the god,
> Go forth, prepare, obey without complaint.
> You are the seed-corn of a new world.
> This is the Sacred Spring which he desires.)

One of the principles of the Union was the equality granted to arts and crafts, another the contact with foreign artists. For example as early as the third exhibition of 1899 there was a Walter Crane Room and a Grasset Room. And the introduction to the fifth exhibition, which was dedicated to drawing, shows even more clearly the path they had taken:

> The true domain of coloured drawing is the decoration of surfaces. The principles of surface decoration and those of the picture are in complete opposition. Whereas surface decoration must leave us in no doubt that it is a surface we see, it is the essence of a picture that the impression of flatness is removed, that the effect is one of space.

As a logical consequence there followed in the sixth exhibition of 1900 a large display of Japanese works of art.

Felician von Myrbach was one of the founder members of the *Secession*. On 25 February 1899 he was made acting Principal and later, on 12 March 1900, Director of the Kunstgewerbeschule (School of Arts and Crafts). Myrbach succeeded in engaging the interest of the progressive Secessionist artists for his school. In April 1899 he engaged Josef Hoffmann, in 1900 Koloman Moser joined the staff, and in 1901 Alfred

Roller. On 3 August 1897 another important institute had changed its director: Arthur von Scala took over the direction of the Royal Imperial Museum of Art and Industry, and he immediately began promoting in this field a reform in arts and crafts. The work of these two men did not long remain unrecognized. At the opening of the winter exhibition of the Museum of Art and Industry, the director of the Ministry of Education, Dr. Ritter von Hartel, stated in the presence of Joseph Maria Olbrich, Otto Wagner, Felician von Myrbach and the entire staff:

> The progressive movement in the field of arts and crafts fascinates us at this moment more than at any other time and in any other field. . . . It is clear to all that arts and crafts are gaining new life and vigour from their renewed inner bond with a changed and revitalized world of fine arts. . . .

In 1898 Otto Wagner was invited on to the board of the Museum of Art and Industry; in the same year an exhibition of Japanese coloured woodcuts was held, and in December 1900 there opened a highly-praised exhibition of the works of Walter Crane, whose theoretical works, newly translated into German, were on the book-shelves of every progressive artist.

The Vienna artists at the turn of the century—and this is one reason for the startling quality of the *Jugendstil*—had been taught drawing in their school-days by a completely new method. This had been instituted in 1873, the year of the Vienna Exhibition, by a Commission presided over by Rudolf von Eitelberg, two of the members being Heinrich von Ferstel and Ferdinand Laufberger. The new syllabuses for free drawing were put into force by a decree of 9 August 1873.

The influence of the English Arts and Crafts Movement on the Viennese *Jugendstil* was particularly important. In the year 1886 Charles R. Ashbee, encouraged by Ruskin and Morris, had gathered together a reading circle of handicraft artists. Drawing classes were added and in 1880 the Guild of Handicraft was founded, which was soon increasing in numbers. But it was Walter Crane who was the central figure of this Arts and Crafts Movement. He founded the Art Workers Guild and then in 1888 organized, together with the Arts and Crafts Exhibition Society an exhibition in which for the first time arts and crafts were granted equal rights with the other arts. In the eighth exhibition of the *Secession* in 1900, Ashbee exhibited 52 works, and there were also 33 works by the Glasgow architect Charles R. Mackintosh and his wife. The Viennese were charmed with the elegance of the Mackintosh works. Their architectural style, with furniture of simple basic design, but with elaborate treatment of the upper areas and delicately decorated small ornamental surfaces, evoked an immediate response: the couple were invited to Vienna by art lovers and they stayed for six weeks. Fritz Waerndorfer, a young banker who was passionately interested in art, became a friend of the Mackintoshes and commissioned them to design a music-room for him, which, together with a dining-room designed by Hoffmann, became a sensation in contrasts. The music-room shows indications of the symbolism so important in the *Jugendstil*, for in it were portrayed *les sept princesses* of the Belgian Maurice Maeterlinck. This is not unimportant, for one of the paths of the *Jugendstil* was to lead via the literature of Symbolism from painting and sculpture to arts and crafts and to a renewal of the inner content of ornament. We have only to think of the artists Khnopff, Toorop and Minne, whose works were also exhibited in the Secessionist period.

In 1901 the *Secession* had decided to interrupt the usual repetitive exhibitions of pictures by an event of a different nature. A room based on a single concept was to be created; painting and sculpture had to conform to its demands. The focal point of this exhibition was to be one outstanding work of art. At this time Max Klinger's Beethoven monument was nearing completion. This work was shown in the fourteenth exhibition of 1902 as a tribute to Klinger, for, as the catalogue, illustrated with original woodcuts, stated: 'he has, by his artistic creativity as well as by his words, brought clarity into our vision of art'. Josef Hoffmann, who had been entrusted with the overall artistic supervision, gave the rooms a monumental character; it was in this connection that Gustav Klimt created his famous Beethoven frieze. In complete harmony with the concept of Klinger's work, the exhibition became a festival of material, with works in compressed concrete and plaster-carving covered in gold leaf, with lead-smelting, embossing, and stencil paintings. In this exhibition as never before, surface decoration approached art crafts; a concept of mosaic-like surface governed by the nature of the material began to emerge. The opening of the exhibition was unconventional: one afternoon the rooms were simply handed over to the creator of the Beethoven statue by a small group of artists. After a speech by the president, Roller, six trumpeters on the first floor of the building played the tune of the 'Lied an die Freude' (Song to joy).

> Ahnest du den Schöpfer, Welt?
> Such ihn überm Stenenzelt,
> Uber Sternen muß er wohnen.
>
> (O World, do you sense your Creator?
> Seek him above the starry firmament,
> Above the stars is his dwelling place.)

The conductor was Gustav Mahler, the director of the State Opera.

As late as 1902 Josef Hoffmann undertook a journey to England to study Ashbee's workshop theory, and he also met there Hermann Muthesius, later to be one of the founders of the German Union of Craft Workers. Fritz Waerndorfer had for a long time been observing the English Arts and Crafts movement, and now he became the financial initiator of an undertaking which lent Viennese art of the time a worldwide importance, the Vienna Workshop, which was established in June 1903 as 'a productive association of art craftsmen in Vienna'. The care with which preparations had been made for this undertaking is indicated by a letter from Waerndorfer to Hoffmann dated March 1903, in which he informs him that Mackintosh, to whom he had written about 'our Vienna metal workshops', with a plea for the utmost discretion, had replied positively, and would visit Muthesius the following week. Mackintosh even wrote, on 17 March 1903, a detailed letter with advice on the founding of the workshops.

Waerndorfer not only became the managing director of the Vienna Workshop, he remained until 1913 its inspiration, and he sacrificed his fortune without hesitation so that the often expensive ideas of his

VIENNESE *JUGENDSTIL*

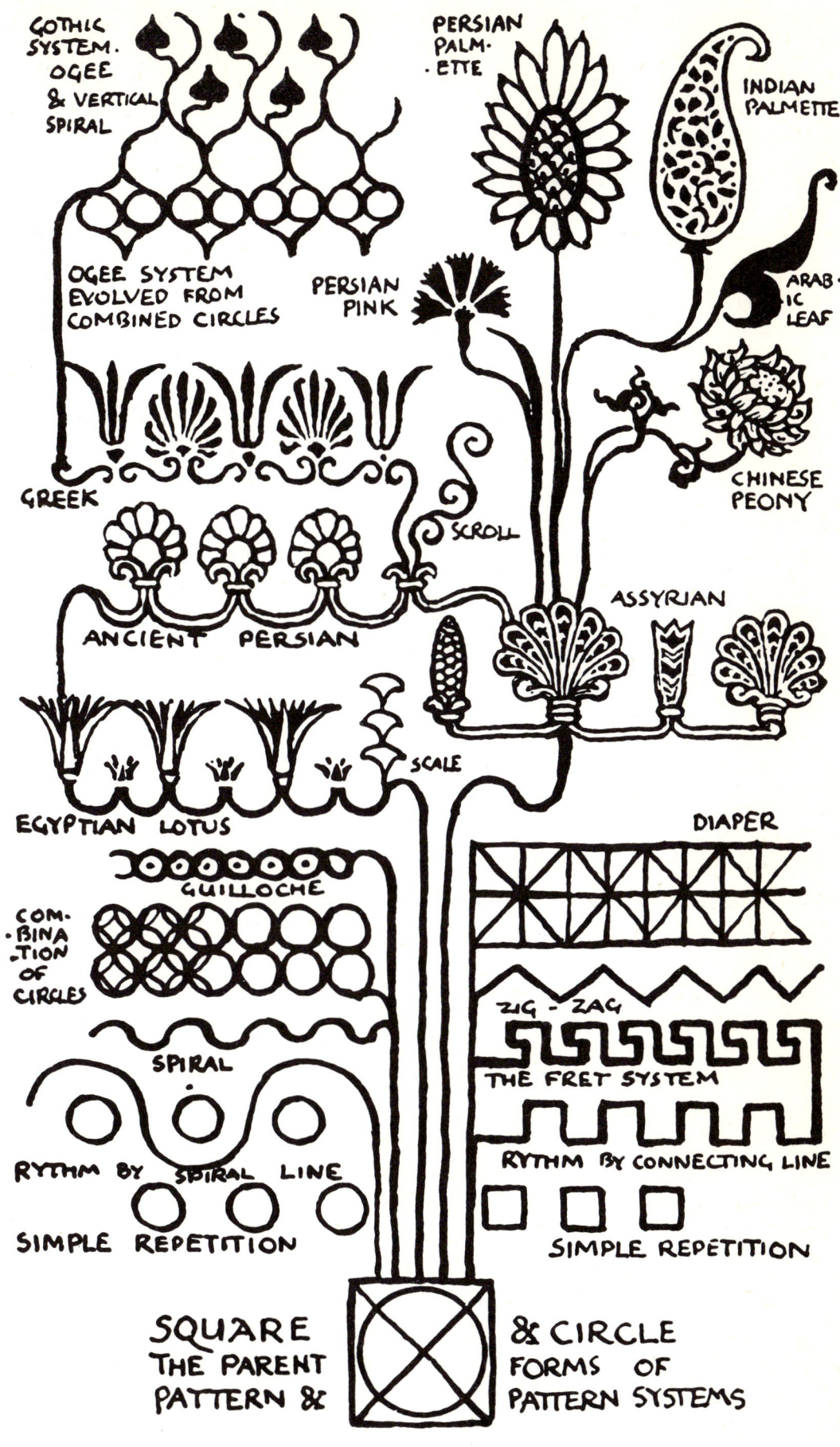

IV. Walter Crane, *Line and Form*, London 1900. P. 89, Tree of typical pattern shapes, units and systems.

artist friends could be put into practice. At first the Workshop executed the designs of the Professors Josef Hoffmann and Koloman Moser only, but other artists were soon recruited. In the workshops the aim was to counteract badly-designed mass-production and the empty imitation of old styles in the sphere of arts and crafts, and to ensure that all objects of everyday use should be artistically designed. Seldom has the concept of a total work of art been developed in such detail as in the creations of the Vienna Workshop.

But what was happening in this period in the *Secession*? Shortly before the foundation of the Workshop, they held an exhibition which corresponded to that other aim of Vienna art of that time, Impressionism. The exhibition was entitled 'The Development of Impressionism in Painting and Sculpture (January–February 1903)'. This project, upon which the organizers had sought the advice of the art historians and critics Richart Muther and Julius Meier-Graefe, is today considered one of the great moments in the history of exhibitions. All the important Impressionists were represented, while amongst the forerunners shown were works by Tintoretto, Vermeer, Velasquez, Delacroix and Corot. There was a separate section composed only of Nabis, with their pattern style based on two-dimensional effect. But the surprising thing in this exhibition was a section of Japanese coloured wood-prints between the Impressionists and the Nabis. The reason for this was given in the introduction to the catalogue.

> Now we come to the newest generation.... Decorative trends are in evidence, there is a yearning for simplification and for style. The Japanese, who, as regards colour, were an inspiration to the Impressionists, once more form a bridge which, first by conscious imitation and later in free individual creativity, leads to the simplifying of the effect of nature.

In the following period the search for style brought about a schism in the Union. Hevesi wrote that the stylists of the Klimt Group had been in favour of a penetration of art into every sphere of life, of an ornamental structuring of our whole existence; arts and crafts played a large part in this. The Impressionists, on the other hand, had held a more exclusive concept of art. Since the two groups could not agree on the form to be taken by future exhibitions, the Klimt Group left the *Secession*.

Naturally the cause of this 'secession from the *Secession*' was the example given by the activities of the Vienna Workshop. In a booklet which they published in 1905, it was stated that:

> We wish to establish a close relationship between the public, the designer and the craftsmen, and to create good, simple household articles. We start with the purpose of the object: our first requirement is its suitability for use, and our strength should lie in sound proportions and good handling of material. We will seek to decorate where this is appropriate, but without compulsion and not for its own sake.... Even we ourselves acknowledge that in certain circumstances a machine can produce a tolerable article, but such an article must inevitably bear the imprint of its manufacture. We do not consider this our province.

The root cause of the resignation lay in business disagreements. Klimt had suggested that the Miethke Gallery be acquired for the *Secession*, in order to place it at the disposal of interested artists, who were allegedly crowded out by too much foreign competition. Paul Bacher, a friend of Klimt, bought the gallery for this purpose. Karl Moll became the artistic director. But this enterprise was condemned by the opposition party.

In the next years the artists of the Klimt Group exhibited their works together with the Vienna Workshop as a matter of course, some even collaborating with the individual workshops. In 1905 the two groups had already combined to hold an exhibition in the newly opened rooms of the Miethke Gallery. This had already become the gallery most favoured by the younger generation. A Beardsley exhibition was held there about 1904. Waerndorfer, who was an enthusiastic collector of this artist's work and even translated his letter in 1908, probably played some part in this.

In 1908 the artists of the Klimt Group had organized an exhibition in conjunction with the Vienna Workshop, an Arts Review in a new hall on the Schwarzenbergplatz built by Josef Hoffmann. The president, as at the beginning of the *Secession*, was Gustav Klimt. In this exhibition there were, as well as new paintings, sculptures and craft works of great excellence, and a room designed by Berthold Löffler which was devoted to poster art. According to the photographs still preserved, the posters exhibited there were among the most beautiful products of ornamental poster art. Unfortunately, very few of these works are found in today's collections.

The artists whose works were shown in the Arts Review were not members of one organization but were united more or less by the conviction expressed by Gustav Klimt in his opening speech: 'No sphere of human existence is too small or unimportant to offer a place for artistic endeavour'.

The Arts Review was a gathering of the most progressive artists of the day. It was joined by two artists of the *Jungbund*, founded in 1902: Czeschka and Powolny. But also, for the first time, a new generation appeared, among them Kokoschka, who gained his first major successes at this exhibition. The Review was repeated in 1909, but the movements it represented had passed their zenith, and the Viennese *Jugendstil* began to give place to a more prosaic concept of art.

THE POSTERS

The early period of Viennese poster art—whose history has not yet been written—was characterized by the text poster, which was often a sort of poster newspaper. Here we must mention in particular the pamphlets of 1848. The importance attached to these by the public of that time is shown by a proclamation issued by the last provisional Head of the Vienna National Guard, the text of which reads:

> During the present period of stress I find it necessary to abstain from the customs of more peaceful times. I may speak openly to the whole population, since in this time of danger we rely on the intelligence of the whole population and on its love of liberty. It is through posters that important news needing to be communicated to all can be most easily disseminated. Success and victory in the field depend on fleeting moments.

Alongside these text posters the picture poster was developing, which in its lithographic form reflected the New Renaissance of the eighties. There were also numerous woodcut posters, of which HANS SCHLIESSMANN's caricatures are the best known. Schliessmann transcended these works, with their restless effect due to over-illustration, by a series of absolutely simple silhouette posters. The art of the silhouette cutters, and silhouette theatre imported from Asia, may have been the inspiration for this. This simplification may have paved the way for the modern concept of the poster, even though the types portrayed were not designed to give the effect of a Japanese composition; they have their origins in a type of illustration which was still preoccupied with comedy of situation. The text in the negative spaces is not balanced; we are also jarred by the man's hat, which cuts into the text, disturbing the two-dimensional effect by giving an impression of depth.

The other early example by HEINRICH LEFLER shows a firm command of the principles of composition in artistic figure posters which had been brought in from abroad; the boyish appearance of the reading woman, the chrysanthemum pattern of the wallpaper, and the consciously fortuitous character of the brief sketch—one might be viewing the scene through a window at sunset—recall its Anglo-American forerunners.

GUSTAV KLIMT produced the poster for the first Secessionist Exhibition. This poster is unprecedented in its composition. It caused a sensation, and not only on account of the empty space which fills the centre of the picture, which is almost a *tabula rasa*. It also demonstrated to the public the awakening of the 'Sacred Spring' of Viennese art. In the upper part of the picture is depicted the battle between Theseus and the Minotaur, watched by Athena, the faithful helper of brave warriors, goddess of wisdom and patroness of the arts. Of course the picture—Theseus is just drawing back to deliver the death blow—was intended to symbolize the battle between the *Künstlerhaus* and the *Secession*. Since the picture outraged the moral sensibilities of the Vienna police, trees had to be superimposed in order to cover Thesus' nakedness.

It is characteristic that the breakthrough to a new poster style did not take place in commercial posters. The art exhibition poster does not advertise, it makes known cultural values. If it is a good poster it contains elements which demonstrate artistic theory; sometimes it is almost a manifesto turned picture. Few pictures give better proof of this statement than the one mentioned above and the poster which ARNOŠT HOFBAUER created for the second exhibition of the Prague Union of Artists, Manes, in the Topićův salon in 1898. This Union, founded as early as 1887, endeavoured to unite all the artistic efforts of the generation of the nineties with the purpose of opening a window on Europe. How very successful the consciously progressive programme of this organization was is shown by the fact that up until 1914 hardly any Czech poster of importance was produced outside the aegis of the organization. The plate reproduced in this book shows the poster without text. A lifebelt is being thrown to a drowning man, who is the focal point of the picture. The ship represents the Union of Artists, Manes, under the sail of the Topićův salon. The drowning man is a young artist who has been overwhelmed by the wave of Hokusai (after the famous woodcut). The Manes Union is the rescuer from the all-pervading Japanese influence of the time.

JOSEPH MARIA OLBRICH not only designed the exhibition rooms of the *Secession*, he composed the poster for the first exhibition which took place in these rooms. The view shows their original state, with the inscription *Ver Sacrum*, which is now missing, and the small round bushes next to the entrance which were so important as a counterbalance to the dome. The building was originally white, the dome and the small decorative pillars were gilded, the background dark blue.

KOLOMAN MOSER's poster for Fromme's Calendar was designed in 1899, and was used until 1914 as the firm's permanent poster. The Norn with the hour-glass and the snake-ring—an ancient emblem denoting the eternal circle of life, and time running out—had appeared even before Moser's poster as an advertising motif for calendar makers. But here the realistic outline surrounds a closed surface, exemplifying the new two-dimensional approach to composition. KOLOMAN MOSER also created the poster for the fifth exhibition of the *Secession* in 1899, on which is seen a winged genius with the badge of the *Secession*. The picture, printed with many variations of colour, was typical of the *Jugendstil*, with flowing curves and tendrils.

As early as 1899 ADOLF KARPELLUS designed the poster for Julius Meinl's Malt Coffee, the text of which might have been written by a modern advertising specialist, so skilful are the statements: 'Nothing can beat the aroma of real coffee' and 'Once you have tasted Julius Meinl's Malt Coffee, you will know it is the best and will drink no other'. The pictorial story of the coffee-drinker who is miming his praise of the coffee strongly resembles a modern comic strip, but here it causes the beholder to read the text. Karpellus, who designed a large number of posters, was one of the few artists who were able to draw on stone, since he had followed the training as a lithographer as was necessary in Austria at that time.

The anonymous poster for the tobacco industry shows how the traditional realistic method of advertising popular with the client could be brightened by the addition of an appealing picture in the modern style. Naturally the young lady has not sampled all the different cigars and cigarettes; whether her function is to provide associations of youth and freshness, in the manner of modern advertising, is not clear.

An important designer of posters at the turn of the century was JOSEF MARIA AUCHENTALLER; his poster for the postcard lottery of

1900 with the goddess Fortuna, whom another author thinks to be Mercury, shows a certain French influence. The first prize was an oil painting by Wilhelm Bernatzik or 2000 crowns. It would be interesting to know whether the winner took the picture or managed to resist this early attempt to influence the price of works of art.

Delightful, too, is the idea of the poster on a poster. One advertisement created in 1902 shows an elegant *danseuse* who is showing on strings numerous poster-marionettes. In the printer's note, two artists' names are given; ERWIN PUCHINGER seems to have been responsible for the total concept, while FERDINAND PAMBERGER lithographed and reproduced the individual elements of the poster. Amongst the poster marionettes we can make out Moser's calendar poster for Fromme which is already known to us. The poster invites its readers to an advertising ball, to which the guests must come dressed as advertising figures. Such advertising balls had been very popular in Europe since 1895, when the first one was given by Alexandre Henriot, the well-known manufacturer of champagne, who was an avid poster-collector.

KOLOMAN MOSER's poster for the thirteenth exhibition of the *Secession* also dates from 1902. In contrast to the posters mentioned above, it shows the modern trends in art exhibition posters, and at the same time demonstrates the effect of Rudolf von Larisch's works in the field of ornamental script-writing. Larisch's demand for the ornamental spacing of letters has been fulfilled in textbook manner in this poster with its geometrical script. Whether the three Muses in their unifying halo really symbolize the desire for a reconciliation of the three Viennese artists' unions of the time (*Künstlerhaus*, *Secession* and *Hagenbund*) or are the personifications of architecture, sculpture and painting, is a question which can no longer be answered.

LEOPOLD BURGER's announcement of the revised performance of Ferdinand Raimund's tragi-comedy *The Fateful Crown or King without a Country, Hero without Courage, Beauty without Youth* shows the use of ornamentation to explain the content of the picture. The play opened on 30 August 1902 in the Imperial Jubilee Theatre, which is today the Opera House.

In an advertisement for gramophones and typewriters, JULIUS KLINGER makes the spectator part of a public impressed by the advances in technology. This very original drawing, in which the objects advertised are almost completely ousted from the centre of attraction by the spectators, is typical of Klinger's early period, which relies to a great extent on humour, but at the same time already contains all those elements which were to determine the future course of this advertising artist towards the functional style of the twenties.

Ornamental puzzle texts with which critics often had to wrestle for a considerable time were particularly popular with artists as a means of surface composition. It is significant that LEOPOLD FORSTNER later opened a workshop for mosaic. A group, the Wiener Kunst im Hause (Viennese Art in the Home), who commissioned one by Forstner to advertise their exhibition, was formed in 1901 by students of the School of Arts and Crafts, who wished by this means to foster renewed interest in arts and crafts. However, the group was never of any real importance.

ORNAMENTAL POSTERS

One of JULIUS KLINGER's most original ideas is the poster for the Third International Motor Exhibition. The little devil's head and its huge shadow distracts the beholder's attention from the subject of motors. One is prompted to question the connection between the devil and motor-cars, and wonder whether to visit this exhibition. Devils were a favourite motif on posters; on the cabaret poster by VIKTOR SCHUFINSKY there is another such delightful figure, its outline rising almost inevitably from the red surface.

The two posters of the 1905 art exhibition are by JOSEF HOFFMANN. They are a good illustration of the austere patterning of the Vienna Workshop, which is sometimes almost heraldic. The text was printed in offset, and the coloured pattern was stencilled in by hand.

LEOPOLD STOLBA's monochrome poster for the twenty-third exhibition of the *Secession* advertised the last event arranged by the Union before the resignation of the Klimt group. Stolba, a great collector of cacti, painted studies of nature with almost scientific precision. A detail to note here is the diagonal division of the picture with the two-dimensional floral pattern in the one part and the impression of depth in the other: a contrast which seems to reproduce visually the contradictory views held by the Engelhart circle and the Klimt group. The poster for the twenty-sixth exhibition of the *Secession* (1906) was designed and lithographed by FERDINAND ANDRI. This ornamental magic mountain representing Spring was one of the attempts to preserve the symbolism of the *Secession* after the resignation of the Klimt group. The Hungarian IMRE SIMAY made the poster for the nineteenth exhibition of the *Hagenbund*. The motif of the man struggling to roll a mighty stone uphill was typical of Hungarian poster art at the time. This picture was also one of the leitmotifs of Hungarian miniature graphic art during the *Jugendstil* period.

BERTHOLD LOFFLER's *Girl's Head* was the main poster advertising the Arts Review 1908. Even before it opened, stamps with the same design had been printed and distributed to those interested. Hevesi wrote:

> The postmen must be the ones best informed on this project, for on many letters now there is a stamp advertising the exhibition in bright blue and yellow. A girl's profile with long gold tresses flowing down over her blue dress. Such ornamentation has not been seen since the very early days of *Ver Sacrum*. It is as stylish as only the impossible can be and more pleasant than any other stamp. And how effective it looks as a stamp! Many post office ladies cannot refrain from cancelling it out!

OSKAR KOKOSCHKA's poster for the same exhibition signifies the transition from Viennese black and white ornamentation to Expressionism. In contrast to the elegant delineation of area in the manner of Löffler, these broken outlines give an effect of torn tissue paper. With these posters for the Arts Review, Kokoschka first showed examples of his art which were popular with the public.

The poster for a 'Sensational Sketch' in the Colosseum was created by REMIGIUS GEYLING in 1908. The drawing has symbolic meaning; amongst the wealth of decorative motifs a bomb is ticking. Ornamentation was outdated, beautiful decoration was suddenly at variance with the technological world around it. Similarly, LEOPOLD FORST-

NER'S poster for the exhibition 'The Modern Office' (1909) is undeniably beautiful to look at, but the typewriter, a purely useful object, does not harmonize very well with its ornamental surroundings.

J. (LAJOS?) BERAN's advertisement for a monoplane (1911) uses a completely new subject for a poster. Such subjects spoke for themselves and required no additional ornamentation. And yet construction, framing and lettering can indubitably be traced back to the ornamental forerunners of these latter-day posters.

This growing trend of functionalism naturally affected also the art exhibition poster, which had to struggle to defend its pre-eminence. On the beautiful text poster by FRANTISEK KYSELA for the thirty-fourth exhibition of the Manes Union, the lettering is suddenly clear and legible.

Ornamental patterns are now frequently placed on an empty background. ERWIN PUCHINGER's poster for the Vienna Union of Arts and Crafts may stand as an example of this trend. The border has vanished, the ornament serves only to accentuate, the large single block begins to predominate.

Meanwhile, many Austrian poster designers had moved to Germany, mainly to Berlin, where under their influence the functional poster began to develop. The poster for the firm of Salamander was designed by ERNST DEUTSCH in Berlin as early as 1912. This poster, too, shows the influence of the Vienna school, in the chequer-board pattern and the thematic repetition of women's legs. But ornamentation had not yet been renounced completely in Vienna, as the posters for the State Lottery designed by RUDOLF JUNK were to demonstrate for some time to come. However, the State Lottery was an undertaking with no competitors which could therefore afford the luxury of adhering to such an old tradition.

The Viennese method of composition can be recognized in the posters of EMIL PIRCHAN, who had moved to Munich. The lettering on his poster, published in 1913, shows traces of Rudolf von Larisch's teaching. JULIUS KLINGER had already been working for some time now in Berlin, but he reintroduced some Viennese decorative motifs in his poster for the Spring Show of 1914. One might almost be viewing an object from the Vienna workshops. This ornamentation, which arose naturally from a solid foundation in Vienna, was in Berlin a costly exotic decoration. The functional concept had temporarily prevailed—although through the Vienna Workshop there was one more blossoming of ornamental patterning. MICHAEL BIRO's poster for the Budapest State Zoo shows the emancipation of the poster from domination by ornamentation, although even here the construction of the negative space around the vulture is a visible proof of the continuance of the Viennese concept of poster art.

THE PLATES

HANS SCHLIESSMANN
Jacobi Antinicotin
c. 1890

An early example of a very original advertisement for the tobacco industry, which declares the harmlessness of the cigarette advertised and at the same time seeks to gain custom amongst schoolboys. The spectator can identify either with the astonished gentleman or with the puffing boys. The figures have their origins in a type of illustration which is still completely preoccupied with comedy of situation. In the eighties Schliessmann designed a whole series of wood-cut caricatures. The art of silhouette cutting, which was at its most popular in the eighteenth century, and also possibly the shadow theatre imported from Asia, seem to have been the inspiration for a whole series of silhouette posters by the artist. Furthermore, his book *Wiener Schattenbilder* (Vienna Silhouette Pictures), containing many situations such as this one, was published in 1892. The script of the poster in the negative spaces is quite unbalanced, particularly in the lower section; and the man's hat strikes a jarring note, since it cuts into the text and thus disturbs the two-dimensional effect by giving an impression of depth.

The Jacobi Anti-nicotine cigarette was apparently an early filter-tip cigarette.

63 × 95·5 cm.

Zincotype. No printer's stamp.

WAS? PAPA

JACOBI AN

This art exhibition poster shows part of a stage, the curtains being cleverly used to frame the picture. There is no interior drawing; the picture is created entirely with blocks of colour.

Like other artists Emil Pirchan had left Austria because conditions of work for artists at the beginning of the century were easier in Germany. One might almost speak of an exodus, so many artists left at this time—to mention but a few, Carl Otto Czeschka, Franz Delavilla, Ernst Deutsch, Karl Kling, Julius Klinger, Oskar Kokoschka, Erwin Lang, Richard Luksch, Emanuel Josef Margold, Franz Metzner, Joseph M. Olbrich, Max Oppenheimer, Emil Orlik, Jo Steiner and Joseph Urban. Some of these artists returned later, amongst them Emil Pirchan, who made a name for himself as an author through his important works on Gustav Klimt and Hans Makart, amongst other works.

122·8 × 92 cm.

Colour lithography.

Print by the Graphic Works, Munich-Eggenfelden.

EMIL PIRCHAN
Emil Pirchan,
Stage Designs
1913

An advertisement for a branded article which is typical of the period. The picture shows that, unlike in former times, one can now even read by the light of a gas lamp, if one uses the new gas mantle. The subdued colours showing the effect of the lamplight lend an intimate tone to the picture, and the realistic portrayal gives the impression of glancing into a window at dusk.

In 1895 the chemist Carl Auer of Welsbach, (b. 1858), invented the gas mantle, or so-called Auer mantle. Previous to this, solid objects like chalk or magnesium had been heated in a gas flame, which was normally only faintly luminous, and caused to glow. To achieve this same effect, Auer introduced a framework of oxidized metal which considerably increased the brightness of the gas flame. The Auer light was not only the cheapest light, but it produced so little heat and carbon dioxide that it was also medically safer. In 1898 Auer manufactured the osmidium metal wire light bulb, and in 1904 Auer metal, a synthetic flintstone for lighters. In 1907 he built the Treibacher Chemical Works near his castle in Carinthia. This was the first factory for the production of thorium and cer.

46·5 × 59 cm.

Colour lithography based on artist's design.

Printed by S. Czeiger, Vienna.

Variants with five trade marks in the border.

HEINRICH LEFLER
Auer Light
after 1895
overleaf

KOLOMAN MOSER

Fromme's Calendar

1899

The permanent poster of a calendar firm, which can be proved to have been used as an advertisement between the years 1899 and 1914. This fact speaks for the efficacy of the design, which was considered very advanced in 1899, with its large-scale portrayal of the motif and the almost complete renunciation of interior drawing. The silhouette of the body is in mysterious contrast to the realistically portrayed head and hands. The unwavering gaze of the woman underlines the symbolism of the design: the Norn with the hour-glass and snake-ring embodies the eternal circle of life and the running out of time. The firm used this poster in a psychologically skilful way to persuade the spectator to an annual disbursement and to link the design in his mind with the particular company.

In 1894 the firm of Carl Fromme was already claiming on a poster to be the oldest and most important calendar merchant in Austria. This poster shows a man with a box which is covered with at least forty different calendars. The dating of our poster is based on an advertisement entitled *Calendars with modern appeal*, which appears in the catalogue for the fifth exhibition of the *Secession* (1899). This offers five different calendars with drawings by Koloman Moser: Fromme's Rhyme and Maxim Calendar, Fromme's Elegant World Calendar and Notebook, Fromme's Stephanie Calendar, Fromme's Luxury Calendar and Fromme's Vienna Purse Calendar. In connection with the last-mentioned we are told it is offered either 'in the usual envelopes or in new ones with delightful modern drawings by Koloman Moser'. The Prints Department of the Albertina has in its possession a Fromme's Rhyme and Maxim Calendar for 1900 designed by Koloman Moser. (Moser, ill. B. 401.206- A.)

95 × 63 cm.

Colour lithography and gold-bronze dusting process from artist's design.

Printed by Albert Berger, Vienna.

The poster was also printed in other colours.

An art exhibition poster with a symbolic picture. This two-dimensional composition swirls around the lifebelt in the centre. The close-up of the head of the drowning man contrasts with the smallness of the figure in the boat. In the background the sail encloses the picture; the viewer's gaze is drawn upward by the wave from the drowning man to the writing on the sail, and then returns diagonally with the life-belt to the drowning man.

This textless poster is an example of the custom particularly prevalent in France at the time of printing special editions of posters without the text in order to sell them as decorations. For the advertising edition the text ran: 'I výstava spolku MANES/od. 3 do 30 listopadu'.
The picture, too, was slightly larger; on the crest on the bows of the boat was written 'SM'. The Prague Artists' Union, Manes, began their exhibitions in the Topićův Salon.

109·2 × 82 cm.

Colour lithography.

No printer's stamp (printed by V. Neubert, Prag-Smichov).

5

ARNOŠT HOFBAUER
Topićův salon
1898

An art exhibition poster whose tall structural pattern not only became the basis for a whole series of later *Secession* posters, it was at the same time a sort of model of architecture in pictures. The study of this picture reveals an inherent connection between the surface of the text block and the body of the architecture. If we regard the upper portion on its own, we have simply a drawing of architecture—the ornamental sketch of the *Secession* building. But taken together with the lower part which with its solid characters and accompanying curves mirrors the fine ornamental lines of the building, it becomes a completed picture and gives to the architecture a sacrosanct, unattainable quality.

The poster shows simply the new *Secession* building—but it thus proclaims the triumph of a group of artists, who earned so much with their first exhibition that they could afford to build themselves an Exhibition Hall. This building was completed within six months and was one of the sights of Vienna, solely on account of the achievement of the artists. In contrast to the first poster, the second has the word 'Secession' in the centre; it now denotes both the artists and their Exhibition Hall.

82·8 × 51·5 cm.

Colour lithography and bronze dusting process from artist's design.

Printed by Albert Berger, Vienna.

For the third exhibition of the *Secession* the same design was used, with different text and colours. The main lines were: 'Secession/Max Klinger/Christ on Olympus/Collection of Const. Meunier/van Rysselberghe' (in above format and also 175 × 70 cm., printed in two parts).

JOSEPH MARIA OLBRICH
Second Exhibition of the *Secession*
1898

This poster for the clothing industry advertises a new fashion in ladies' shoes with high heels, and coming well up on the ankle, which were to be worn with long skirts. The rhythmic repetition of the motif, which covers the whole area, has a lively effect; the contrast of red and green opposes the colour—non-colour contrast (grey particularly, but also black and white are used). The trade mark is effectively positioned in the corner next to the name of the firm with its clear lettering. This lettering, in contrast to the free script of the turn of the century, gives the impression of type. The chequer-board pattern and the thematic repetition of the motif show the influence of the Vienna School. The artist had used the basic idea of this poster once before, when on a poster for the College of Tailoring he had drawn three ladies marching along shouldering their scissors.

This poster is an important example of the new concept of the functional, larger scale poster which developed around 1910 in Berlin, where progressive Viennese artists such as Klinger, Deutsch and Steiner were working. They made a valuable contribution to this new development in style.

7

ERNST DEUTSCH
Salamander
1912
preceding pages

70 × 95 cm.

Colour lithography from artist's design.

No printer's stamp (probably printed by Reklameverlag Ernst Marx, Berlin, advertising publishers).

A text poster in the old Vienna tradition, with a story in pictures to encourage the viewer to read the text. Each picture corresponds to the text beside it. The coffee cups seem intended to break up the monotony of the text, but on a closer inspection—which is necessary for the reading of the text—they exert subliminal pressure on the viewer.

In 1889 Julius Meinl (1869–1944) entered the coffee firm founded by his father, and built it up until they were the provision dealers with the greatest number of branch stores in the Austro-Hungarian Empire. Coffee substitutes had been in use since the seventeenth century. The barleycorns in the advertisement indicate that this malt coffee is made of lightly-malted, moderately-roasted barley with a sugar coating.

8

ADOLF KARPELLUS
Julius Meinl's
Malt Coffee
1899

121·5 × 86 cm.

Colour lithography.

Printed by Laurenz Schlager, Vienna.

NICHTS
ERREICHT DAS KÖSTLICHE AROMA DES ECHTEN
BOHNENKAFFEES.
NICHTS
GEWÄHRT EINEN DERARTIGEN GENUSS UND ÜBT EINEN SOLCHEN WOHLTHÄTIGEN EINFLUSS AUF DEN MENSCHLICHEN ORGANISMUS WIE EINE TASSE VON GUTEM, ECHTEN
BOHNENKAFFEE.
WER ABER AUS IRGEND EINER URSACHE IN SEINEM HAUSHALTE MALZKAFFEE ENTWEDER VERMISCHT MIT ECHTEM KAFFEE ODER UNVERMISCHT FÜR KINDER ANWENDET, DER NEHME IM EIGENEN INTERESSE JA KEINEN ANDEREN ALS:

JULIUS MEINL's MALZKAFFEE

P.S. WER EINMAL JULIUS MEINL's MALZKAFFEE GEKOSTET HAT, WEISS, DASS DIES DER BESTE IST UND WIRD KEINEN ANDERN MEHR TRINKEN.

NIEDERLAGEN von JULIUS MEINL AUSSER DER CENTRALE u. COMPTOIR nur: I. FLEISCHMARKT 7 BEFINDEN SICH IN WIEN: FILIALEN:

This is an advertisement produced for the tobacco industry which attracts the attention with the portrait of a girl, who is surrounded with descriptions of cigars similar to those in a catalogue. The complicated process needed to print the central picture—ten years earlier such a picture would have required at least five plates in colour lithography—shows the development of the techniques which were used in printing in the mid-nineteenth century to reproduce half-tones. A photograph may have served as the original. Even at this early date the tobacco industry's custom of suggesting oral enjoyment by use of the tobacco colour is in evidence.

The picture stands as an example of those numerous anonymous posters found in every collection. The Tobacco Authority, a State enterprise entrusted with the administration of the tobacco monopoly, was established by a tobacco patent of Joseph II in 1784, although as early as 1662, with the *Tabak-Appalto*, the State had claimed the right to hold the monopoly of the import, manufacture and sale of tobacco.

95 × 65·1 cm.

Colour lithography.

Print from the Steyrmühl, Vienna.

9

ANONYMOUS (MONOGRAMME A.K.)
Tobacco Authority
c. 1900

KAIS. KÖN. ÖSTERR. TABAK-REGIE

Bemerkenswerte Zigarren- und Zigarettenmarken der österr. Tabakregie.

Coronas[2] 12 h
Dicke, größere Gestalt, ovaler Querschnitt (plakiert), Goldmundstück, hochfeine Qualität.

Dames[2] 6 h
Elegante Sorte mit Mundstück und Monogramm, sehr leichte Beschaffenheit.

Egyptische III[3] 6 h
Mundstücklose Zigarette von ovalem Querschnitt und sehr milder Beschaffenheit.

Nil[1] 7 h
Erstklassige plakierte Zigarette ohne Mundstück, von hochfeinem, mildem Geschmacke.

Memphis[1] 5 h
Mundstücklose, gut aromatische, leichte Sorte.

Kaiser[1] 4 h
Mundstückzigarette von besonders zarter, angenehmer Qualität.

Sport[1] 3 h
Sehr beliebte, mundstücklose Sorte von guter Qualität (Volkszigarette).

Princesas[3] 6 h
Mundstückzigarette von gefälliger Fasson und aromatischem Charakter.

Selectos[2] 22 h
Nikotinschwache Zigarre modernster Ausstattung, sehr fein und leicht (Diätzigarre).

Ideales[3] 90 h
Hochfeine, gehaltvolle Havanazigarre inländischer Produktion (Dinerzigarre).

Graciosas[3] 30 h
Modern fassoniert, fein und leicht.

Trabuco[1] 18 h
Kleine, sehr gefällige Fasson, mittelkräftig, von Qualitätsrauchern bevorzugt.

Feine Virginier[1] 11 h
Von starken Rauchern gesuchte Zigarre von besonderer Fasson und eigenartigem Charakter.

Britanica[1] 16 h
Große, mittelkräftige Sorte von keulenähnlicher Form.

Regalia media[3] 20 h
Mittelgroß, zylindrisch geformt, feiner, leichter Charakter.

Anmerkung.
1) Nur im allgemeinen Verschleiße erhältlich.
2) Nur im Spezialitäten-Verschleiße erhältlich.
3) Allgemein erhältlich.

„Steyrermühl", Wien.

This art exhibition poster is more austere than the other by Hoffman, which was designed at the same time. It has a simple surface pattern. The basic element of this pattern resembles a helmet: it reminds one of heraldic models, since the geometrically divided crests used in heraldry—the so-called herald's pictures—were constructed on similar principles.

The Vienna Workshop was founded in May 1903 by the banker Fritz Waerndorfer and the Professors Josef Hoffmann and Koloman Moser of the School of Arts and Crafts. The workshops were established in June 1903 as 'the *Wiener Werkstätte*, a productive association of art craftsmen in Vienna'. Initially, they executed only designs by Josef Hoffmann and Koloman Moser, but from the beginning of 1905 they also called on other collaborators, and in the ensuing period became an artists' association, and functioned as a centre for the Klimt group, which had left the *Secession*. Some of the most important fruits of this co-operation were the Palais Stoclet in Brussels, numerous other buildings which were conceived as total works of art and also the Arts Review 1908 and the International Art Show 1909. The workshops lasted until 1932, when they were closed for financial reasons. Through the opening of the Fledermaus Night-club in the Kärntnerstrasse 33, in October 1907, the W.W. also enriched the Vienna theatre world. In November 1907 it opened a sales office and in May 1909 another in Karlsbad (Haus Pelikan, Alte Wiese), where there was also a second for some time. The development of the W.W. and its supreme importance in arts and crafts can best be seen by enumerating the W.W sales offices opened at later dates:

Kärntnerstrasse 32 (materials and lamps).
Kärntnerstrasse 41 (fashions)
Central office: Vienna I, Tegetthoffstrasse 7–9
Berlin office: Berlin-W, Kronenstrasse 71, later Friedrich-Ebert-Strasse 2–3
Marienbad, Haus Merkur
Zürich, Bahnhofstrasse 1
Lucerne, Haldenstrasse 7
New York, 581 Fifth Avenue
Trieste, Via di Scocola 495 (Italian General Agency)

90·5 × 61·8 cm.

Offset lithography from artist's design. Stencils by artist.

No printer's stamp. (Chwala's print, Vienna, or Albert Berger, Vienna.)

10

JOSEF HOFFMANN
Vienna Workshop
(blue)
1905

OSKÉ
ĚENÍ
VA S.V.U
VIL u ZÁHŘ
?–PROSIN

U. NEUBERT SMÍCHOV

The Prague Artists' Union, Manes, made more and more use of text posters in its advertising of exhibitions. Like this example, they show particularly clearly the increase in functional posters and the decline in ornamental style towards the end of the first decade of the twentieth century. A typical poster technique is the insertion of the sticker which makes the 'Thirty-third' exhibition into 'Thirty-fourth'.

This exhibition of Swedish art had previously been on view at the Exhibition Rooms of the *Hagenbund,* which was extending its traditional contacts with Czech, Hungarian and Polish artists as far as Scandinavia.

94·5 × 125·5 cm.

Colour lithography.

Printed by V. Neubert, Prag-Smichov.

FRANTIŠEK KYSELA
Svedske Umeni
1911
preceding pages

An art exhibition poster which has as its theme a complicated allegory on the subject of art. Its effectiveness comes from the contrast between flat surface and depth. The empty surface in the middle has two values: from the point of view of text it is a writing surface, from the point of view of the figures it becomes a wall, thus giving a gradation in depth. Athena on the right seems to stand on the text block; she is all sculpture, as opposed to the painting of the wall picture on the architecture. In the upper picture Theseus is about to deliver the death blow to the Minotaur. The poster is painting above, text picture below; to the right the representation of the Gorgon's head on the shield of the goddess is an emblem to ward off evil. Depth and surface meet in the signature. The trees were printed in later, to cover Theseus' nakedness, which had outraged the censors.

This poster announced to the public the first exhibition of the Union of Creative Artists of Austria, and also publicized their magazine *Ver Sacrum*. The picture represents the struggle between the *Künstlerhaus* and the *Secession*.

96 × 69 cm.

Colour lithography and bronze dusting process, based on artist's design.

Printed by Albert Beyer, Vienna.

Variations in format: 63·5 × 47 cm. (pink), 40 × 29·5 cm. (olive green). From the same design also came a poster for *Ver Sacrum* with a black text, 52·3 × 37·3 cm. All these variants stamped by censor.

Preliminary sketch in the Vienna Historical Museum.

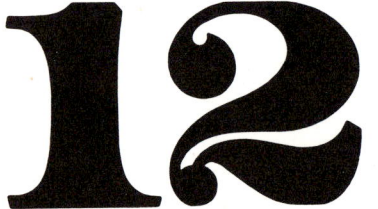

GUSTAV KLIMT
First Exhibition of the *Secession*
1898

BERTHOLD LÖFFLER

Arts Review,
Vienna 1908

1908
preceding pages

This art exhibition poster has a particular charm in that within the narrow strip of the picture the viewer's gaze is drawn to the left and to the girl's face away from the normal direction for reading. Her face, hair and dress prevent any perception of depth; the profile, underlining the two-dimensional concept, the waving lines of the hair on the coloured surface, and the scatter-pattern of the crosses on the dress are all in the same plane as the lettering. The directing of the eye to the left is reinforced by the letters, some of which lean slightly to the left (particularly the 's'). The design was also used for advertising stamps, which were no less striking than the poster.

In co-operation with the Vienna Workshop, the Klimt group held an Arts Review in new Exhibition Rooms built by Josef Hoffmann on the Schwarzenbergplatz. The president, as at the beginning of the *Secession*, was Gustav Klimt. The contents of one room, designed by Berthold Löffler, consisted exclusively of ornamantal posters. The designers included Franz Delavilla, Leopold Forstner, Rudolf Kalvach, Anton Kling, Oskar Kokoschka, Erwin Lang, Koloman Moser, Viktor Schufinsky, Eduard Wimmer. There were no posters by Julius Klinger on show, but several of his ornamental drawings.

68 × 96 cm.

Printed by Albert Berger, Vienna.

Format variant: 34 × 47·5 cm.

It was also used before and during the exhibition as an advertising stamp.

The original is in the Historical Museum of the City of Vienna.

VIKTOR SCHUFINSKY

Lucifer

c. 1904
left

This advertisement for a night-club is reminiscent of the French poster advertisements of the turn of the century, where the portrayal of the milieu of the *demi-monde* was especially popular. In contrast to such posters, this one is strongly abstract, although this does not detract from the erotic quality of the picture. The format, which cuts off the sides of the design, is unusually tall and narrow, and the ornamental line-drawing of the figure of this devil seems to rise almost inevitably from the coloured surface, giving a stained glass effect. By rejecting the use of colour in the body, the artist has skilfully been able to exploit the contrast between the coloured and the white areas.

This poster is the only reminder of this night-club which is still extant.

180 × 60 cm.

Colour lithography, printed in two parts.

Printed by Albert Berger, Vienna.

A poster advertising an event, based on the unusual idea of showing famous posters as marionettes in the hands of a dancer. On the right we can recognize Koloman Moser's design for Fromme's Calendar. Above, left, is a reversed image of Alfred Roller's permanent poster with the winged genius, who as the personification of the mountain railway is carrying people up the mountain on his back. The dancing couple and the Turk rolling a cigarette were two famous posters advertising Le Griffon cigarette paper. Some of the pictures with texts are self-explanatory. The picture of a back being rubbed (next to the dancer, on the right) is taken from a poster by Josef Pfeiffer advertising Brázay's brandy. Below right, the newspaper-boy is carrying a *Neue Freie Presse* under his arm. Some of the posters are no longer identifiable today.

15

ERWIN PUCHINGER AND FERDINAND PAMBERGER

Advertising Ball

1900

The first known advertising ball took place in Reims in 1895 at the house of the champagne manufacturer and collector of posters, Alexandre Henriot. There is also evidence that such balls took place in Berlin between 1896 and 1900.

The double printer's stamp (right, below the picture, and left, under the text) leads us to believe that the upper part may have been used on its own, or with another text. The poster is to a certain extent also an example of the 'collective advertising' so popular at the turn of the century for notices.

Carl Michael Ziehrer (1843–1922), composer of operettas, had been permanent band master of the Hoch- und Deutschmeister Regiment No. 4 since 1884, and from 1908–1918 he was to be the last musical director of court balls.

Carl Wilhelm Drescher (1850–1925) had been an independent band leader and music director since 1874; he composed over two hundred pieces.

The advertising agency of Julius Endlicher—whose firm is mentioned on a poster next to the newspaper-boy—was founded in Florisdorf and owned six hundred hoardings in Vienna.

166 × 83·5 cm.

Colour lithography by Ferdinand Pamberger from a design by Erwin Puchinger, printed in two parts.

Printed by the Society for Graphic Art Industry, Vienna.

The strong geometric element in the composition of this art exhibition poster reveals the structure of the screen base. The architectural quality of the construction, with its tall format, the square motif so important in further developments and the unity of picture and text produced by the diagrammatic character of the composition prove, in contrast to Moser's poster for the fifth exhibition, that a change in the concept of surface had taken place in Vienna. Whether the three Muses in their unifying halo really symbolize a desire for a reconciliation of the three Vienna Artists' Unions (*Künstlerhaus, Secession* and *Hagenbund*) or are merely personifications of architecture, sculpture and painting, it is now impossible to say.

The thirteenth exhibition showed a collection from the Munich Group of artists known as Die Scholle (Native Earth). The main picture of the exhibition, however, was Arnold Böcklin's *Meeresidylle* (Sea Idyll) of 1887, which was bought by the Ministry of Education for the new Modern Gallery. Pictures by Franz von Stuck were also shown. Koloman Moser not only designed the poster but also the catalogue and the entire interior decoration for this exhibition. Photographs which have been preserved show the use of squares and of triangular friezes in the decoration of the walls.

95 × 31·5 cm.

Colour lithography from the artist's design.

Printed by Albert Berger, Vienna.

Format variants: 187 × 63·5 cm.

16

KOLOMAN MOSER

Thirteenth Exhibition of the *Secession*

1902

This is a theatre poster with rich linear ornamentation which helps to elucidate the content. It depicts the main character in the play, the tailor Zitternadel, the Hero without Courage. The scissors next to him are a stage property, but at the same time indicate the possibility of a courageous confrontation of the Fate before which the tailor trembles. The lines surrounding him are the spiritual symbol of the evil which has possessed the magic crown. The text is arranged under the almost calligraphic lines. The tragi-comic character of the play is expressed by the contrast between the ghost bearing the crown and the frightened tailor caught fast in the ornamentation.

The Kaiser-Jubiläums-Theater (Imperial Jubilee Theatre) was built in 1898 on the occasion of the fiftieth anniversary of the accession of the Emperor Franz Josef I, from plans by the architects Franz von Krauss and Alexander Graf. The clients, a Vienna Citizens' Association founded in 1895, wished to give the theatre a Germanic character by use of the German Renaissance style, but in as unusual a manner as possible. The façade is decorated with sculptures by Ottmar Schimkowitz, a portrait of the Emperor by Edmund Hofmann von Aspernburg and twelve reliefs by Georg Leisek. The opening night was 14 December 1898. Ferdinand Raimund's magic play, entitled *The fateful Crown, or King without a Country, Hero without Courage, Beauty without Youth* originally had two acts and was accompanied by music by Josef Drechsler. The première on 4 December 1829 in the Theater in der Leopoldstadt—with Ferdinand Raimund playing the main part—got very bad reviews, and the play was not put on again until the new revised version advertised in this poster, which was arranged by the director of the Stadt-Theater, Adam Müller-Guttenbrunn. The new version had four acts and music by Paul Metrosi, and was a great success. This performance took place on Saturday 30 August 1902.

95 × 63·2 cm.

Colour lithography from the artist's design.

Print from the Society for Graphic Art Industry, Vienna.

LEOPOLD BURGER
The Fateful Crown
1902

This art exhibition poster in mosaic style, the lettering of which seems completely illegible at first glance, may have had a plaster cast as the original—a method of design for ornamental script which was touched on in Rudolf von Larisch's course. The bands of silver seem to lie on the surface of the poster as though on a sheet of glass. The script block and the picture are tall, in contrast to the two small side blocks flanking them. The mosaic-tiled hair of the women is an original touch, and the reduction of colour to silver alone, lying free above the drawing, is a daring innovation.

The Union, Vienna Art in the Home, was formed in 1901 by students of the School of Arts and Crafts, and exhibited for the first time that year in the Hanusch Room of the Society of Arts and Crafts. In November 1902 they showed work at the fifteenth exhibition of the *Secession*. The exhibition announced here is the only exhibition known to have taken place on the Union's own premises. Collections of its work were also seen at the twenty-sixth exhibition of the *Secession* in 1906 and in the Exhibition of Austrian Arts and Crafts 1909–1910, which took place in the Austrian Museum of Art and Industry. Particular publicity was given to the organization's stall at the Vienna Christmas market.

18

LEOPOLD FORSTNER

Vienna Art in the Home

1903?

95 × 63·5 cm.

Colour lithography and dusting process from the artist's design.

Printed by Albert Berger, Vienna.

The particular charm of this poster announcing the Motor Exhibition lies in the inspired impudence of the silhouetted devil's head which almost eclipses the motor car. The small head with its huge shadow is an optical puzzle which corresponds to the riddle as to the connection between devil and Motor Exhibition. Not many clients would have had the courage to permit such a surrealistic deviation from the original purpose of the advertisement.

This exhibition, like the first Vienna Motor Exhibition in 1899, was held at the Gardeners' Association, where in 1898 the *Secession* had held its first exhibition. This was an Association which had been founded in 1837 in Vienna, and which started by holding annual exhibitions. In 1863 the Gardeners' Association Building, designed by the architect August Weber, was built on what was later to be the Parkring. It was originally intended only for exhibitions, but after the opening of the Flower Halls was used also for balls, concerts and other events.

126 × 85 cm.

Colour lithography from artist's design.

Variations in format with additional text which announced that the exhibition was organized by the Austrian Automobile Club and was to take place in the rooms of the Gardeners' Association.

19

JULIUS KLINGER
Third International Motor Exhibition
1903

The lettering of this art exhibition poster was designed by the artist and printed in advance on the sheet by the printers. The artist then stencilled in the rest of the poster by hand. The somewhat ragged edges of the red surfaces are an indication of the stencilling, because here the colour brushed on over the stencil has seeped under the edges. The upper portion of the poster with the four-cornered drops gives the impression of a curtain, and this impression is reinforced by the zigzag of the lower edge against the black surface, and the corresponding lower line of the vertical rows of red shapes. A set of black drops has been omitted on the left; the slight irregularity of this constantly repeated surface pattern creates the lively effect of patterned material.

This poster, along with the other by Hoffman reproduced here, and about forty more of which we have only copies, were created for a sort of internal poster competition of the Vienna Workshop. Apparently the originals in the exhibition of the Vienna Workshop, which took place in the newly-opened rooms of the Miethke Gallery, were used to induce visitors to the exhibition to visit also the firm's own premises in the Neustiftgasse. A W.W. brochure which had already been handed out in 1905 to the participants of an 'art stroll' as they visited the Vienna Workshop seems to have been designed for this exhibition as well; this poster is shown on the cover. Exactly the same design as that of the text block was used for the advertisement of the W.W. in the catalogue of the seventeenth exhibition of the *Hagenbund* (November 1905–January 1906).

90·2 × 63 cm.
Offset lithography from artist's design. Pattern hand-stencilled by artist.
No printer's stamp (Chwala's print, Vienna or Albert Berger, Vienna).

JOSEF HOFFMANN
Vienna Workshop
(red)
1905

The plain black and white ornamentation of the blossom is enhanced by the grey of the sky and the lettering. The blossoms form a floral surface pattern on the same level as the lettering, which is set into the framing. Only the grey of the sky gives an impression of depth. The negative spaces seem to contradict the teaching of Rudolf von Larisch, with the strange, simplified lettering and the deliberate unevenness between letters. The varied possibilities of lithography with its contrast between chalk and ink have been skilfully used here to avoid any sense of monotony in this monochrome poster.

This exhibition of the *Secession* was the last one before it was split by the resignation of the Klimt group. The most important exhibits were works by Otto Wagner, who showed models of the Post Office Savings Bank, the Emperor Franz Josef Civic Museum, and the Church of the Lower Austrian State Sanatorium. Another notable exhibit was entitled *A Waiting Room*, and was designed by Emil Hoppe, Marcel Kammerer and Otto Schüntal. Stolba was a member of Engelhart's circle; in November 1900 Hevesi proclaimed him 'a discovery, not to say an invention of Engelhart'. It is strange that Stolba, who had played an important part in the meetings of the *Hagenbund,* did not come to the *Secession* through Engelhart until 1900.

21

LEOPOLD STOLBA

Twenty-third Exhibition of the *Secession*

1905

96 × 64·5 cm.

Lithography from artist's design.

Printed by Albert Berger, Vienna.

This portrayal of physical endeavour is typical in Hungarian poster art. The body line of the man struggling to roll a heavy stone uphill defines the arrangement of surfaces in the rectangular picture. The man seeming to press against the falling diagonal is a skilful linking of form and content in the picture.

In contrast to the *Secession*, which was receptive to all outside influences, the *Hagenbund* interested itself more in the cultivation of the art of its native land. The *Hagenbund* arose from a round table of artists in the Blaues Freihaus, and were called after the proprietor of that restaurant. After the founding of the *Secession* and its first great successes, the artists' group *Hagenbund* was formed, which established itself as an independent organization within the Association of Creative Artists of Vienna, the *Künstlerhaus*. In November 1900 the *Hagenbund* left the *Künstlerhaus* and in January 1902 they held their first exhibition on their own premises, Zedlitzgalle 6.

22

IMRE SIMAY

Nineteenth Exhibition of the *Hagenbund*

1906

100 × 80 cm.

Colour lithography from artist's design.

Printed by Christoph Reisser's Sons, Vienna.

A single advertisement for two branded luxury objects. The unusual picture almost gives the impression of a glimpse of a technical exhibition. These original characters block our view of the novel technical objects displayed; the beholder as it were places himself in the second row and joins the spectators who are respectfully eyeing the means of communication on display. The trade marks remove any lingering doubts as to the importance of the novelties advertised here.

In 1887 Emil Berliner invented the gramophone in Washington. This differed from Edison's phonograph in its use of a flat disc instead of a metal cylinder. The German Gramophone Company in Berlin manufactured these speaking-machines in various forms, and sold them under the Angel brand. The Lambert typewriter with the letter dial was one of the many machines without keys which were undeniably cheap, but which succumbed to competition from the machines with keys.

23

JULIUS KLINGER

Gramophone

c. 1902
overleaf

94·2 × 126 cm.

Colour lithography from artist's design.

Printed by J. Weiner, Vienna.

Variants in form with different texts: 46·2 × 62·5 cm.

GRAMM

SCHUTZMARKE

OSKAR KOKOSCHKA

Arts Review,
Vienna 1908

1908

This poster is characteristic of Kokoschka's transition at that time from black and white ornamentation of the Vienna *Jugendstil* to his own, highly individual, mode of expression. It is a narrative picture, with the effect of a fairytale illustration. A shy young girl is standing in a garden. Her eyes closed, she enjoys the scent of a flower which she has plucked from an unreal-looking plant. The drawing is kept to a minimum with only an occasional black outline. This line is broken; the lack of any interior drawing causes the coloured surfaces to give the impression of torn tissue paper. The free lettering seems to have been carved with a fretsaw; the letters lean on each other and resemble the interval texts in a shadow theatre.

A short time before, Kokoschka had completed for the Vienna Workshop his fairytale *Die Träumenden Knaben* (The dreaming boys). Like this poster the book was connected stylistically with the coloured shadow theatre figures which he created for the Fledermaus Nightclub of that organization. Those arranging the Arts Review, who as Professors of the School of Arts and Crafts were introducing their students there, had granted Oskar Kokoschka a special position by allowing him to design a poster. (Another poster with a similar motif and construction, but more disciplined in execution, was designed by the pupil Rudolf Kalvach.) Even in this exhibition Kokoschka caused a storm, and continued to provoke interest with his drama *Murderer's Hope of Women* and his comedy for automata entitled *Sphinx and Scarecrow*. When this was performed on 4 July 1909 at the Garden Theatre of the International Art Show, the last play to be performed on this open-air stage, fighting broke out among the audience.

94·7 × 63 cm.

Colour lithography.

Printed by Albert Berger, Vienna.

The entire picture of this art exhibition poster is ornamentally stylized and the white of the paper itself is cunningly utilized in its composition. The lower line of lettering serves as a frame for the window of the picture with its magic view; the upper line has been incorporated into the picture and supports the flower boxes in front of the window. The great triangle of the mountain with the regular rhythmical rise of the points of the old and new growth of the conifers forms a zigzag motif in contrast to the wavy motif of the sky. The sky pattern is ambivalent: at one time we seem to see only the white positive shapes, at another, only the black negative shapes. At the top, the red colour is simply contour, but lower down it takes over the function of negative shape from the black. This dynamic composition, so bewildering to the beholder, is a precursor of today's Op art.

This poster by the President of the *Secession* indicates that some of the members of the *Secession* were still interested in the continuance of the *Ver Sacrum* symbolism, even after the resignation of the Klimt group (Josef Auchentaller, Wilhelm Bernatzik, Adolf Böhm, Adolf Hölzel, Josef Hoffmann, Franz W. Jäger, Gustav Klimt, Max Kurzweil, Wilhelm List, Richard Luksch, Franz Metzner, Carl Moll, Emil Orlik, Alfred Roller and Otto Wagner). The *Secession* published for this exhibition a folder with graphic art work in a format of 40×50 cm. (including a coloured lithograph by Ferdinand Andri, entitled *Spring*). In the actual exhibition, besides works by the members, works by the Polish Artists' Union, Sztuka, were also shown, and—among other arts and crafts—a collection from Vienna Art in the Home. Ferdinand Andri may have received the inspiration for this poster from the end-paper for the catalogue for the fourteenth exhibition of the *Secession*, which was designed by Alfred Roller.

89·4 × 59·5 cm.

Colour lithograph from artist's design.

Printed by Alfred Berger, Vienna.

FERDINAND ANDRI

Twenty-sixth Exhibition of the *Secession*

1906

This is a theatre poster which seeks to symbolize the dramatic character of the play, a 'sensational sketch'. The picture and the text block are skilfully linked by the X, which forms a part of the diagonal lines of the picture, and by the letters which seem to rise from the smoke of the bomb. The lower half of the picture contains typical examples of the decorative motifs of the Vienna *Jugendstil*. Stylized flowers in very similar shapes were produced by the Vienna Workshop, and the decorative border of the picture is also typical of Vienna art of the time.

The Colosseum, which was situated in the Nussdorferstrasse, was built in 1899 by R. Stephann, and was used for festivals, balls and concerts. After reconstruction, the main hall, which could seat about six hundred persons, was also used as a theatre. The exterior of the building was decorated in the German Renaissance style, with a baroque interior. Remigius Geyling worked from 1911–1913 and from 1922–1945 as Stage Manager in the Vienna Burgtheater, and from 1913–1922 he was Director of the Society for Stage and Film Art. He invented stage projection, which in 1922 was used for the first time in the Burgtheater, and he created sets for more than four hundred plays and some films.

124·5 × 93·8 cm.

Colour lithography from artist's design.

Printed by J. Weiner, Vienna.

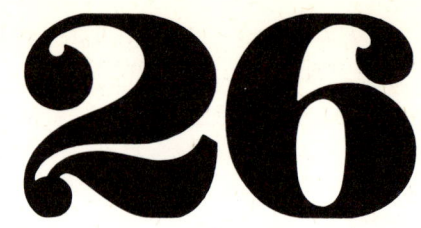

26

REMIGIUS GEYLING

Colosseum: Princess X

c. 1908

This notice of an event has an extremely tall format and is surrounded by a white frame to make it stand out from all the other coloured posters on the hoarding. The format utilizes the whole length of the advertising pillar, excluding the possibility of distraction from other posters. The space in the picture is divided in two in order to create an immediate before and after association in the mind of the beholder through the crabbed book-keeper in his cobwebs and the modern office fairy with her typewriter.

This is another early attempt at advertising typewriters which shows the difficulty experienced by designers in finding a suitable form for advertising modern industrial products.

188 × 63 cm.

Colour lithography, printed in two parts.

Printed by Albert Berger, Vienna.

27

LEOPOLD FORSTNER

The Modern Office

1909

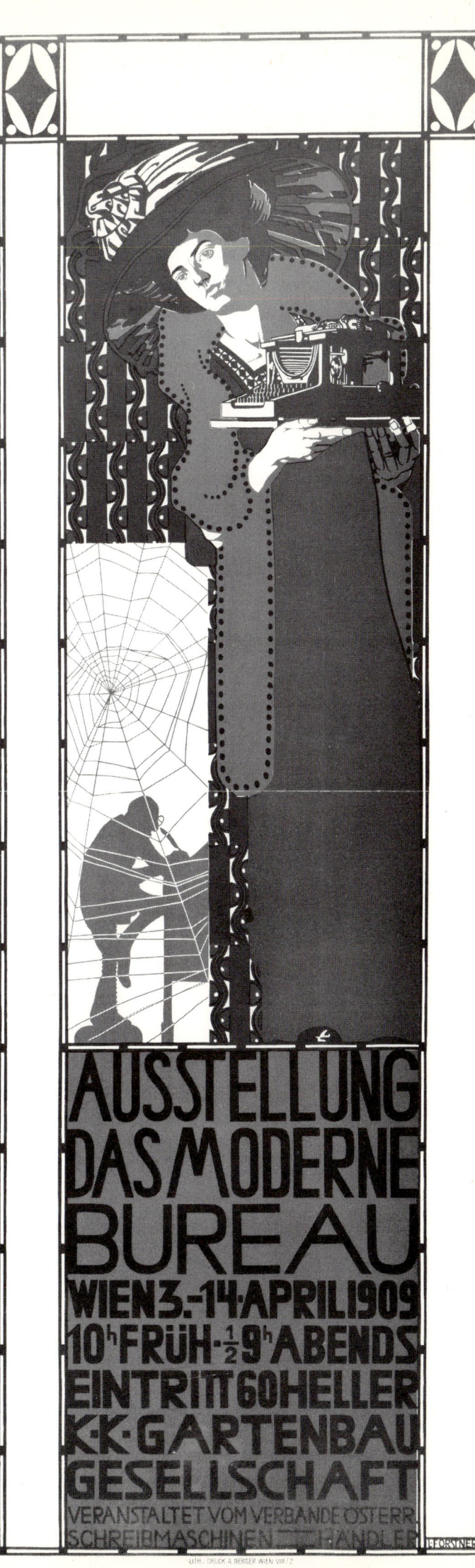

In this notice of an event, the interest lies in the new functional approach, which almost completely does away with ornamentation. Only by the frame and the lettering are we still reminded of that theory of construction which formed the basis of the style of the ornamental poster. The height at which the aeroplane is flying is indicated by the smallness of the mountain inn. The silhouette of this bird of technology was sensation enough in the world of poster art, and needed no further ornamental decoration. The layout of the poster suggests that it may have been used in small format an an advertising stamp.

Igo Etrich, who had applied as early as 1905 for patents for aeroplane propeller and wing designs, built the first Austrian motor-driven aeroplane in 1907, and then in 1910 the Etrich Dove, a single-decker which is shown on this poster. It seems that at this period Etrich was carrying out several such flights—probably in order to finance his projects. For example, on 25 June 1911 he set off in the Etrich Dove—the Etrich monoplane—from the Simmeringer Heath.

28

J. BERAN
Etrich Monoplane
1911

126 × 95 cm.

Colour algraphy.

Print from the Institute for Graphic Art, Stiepel Bros., Reichenberg.

This art exhibition poster deliberately omits the border for the picture and places the stylized drawing immediately against the background surface. An elegant lady, with a flower which is abstract to the point of resembling a sign in her raised left hand, is standing before a bust of Athena. This is modelled on a statue in front of the Vienna Parliament. Ornament is used in this picture only for emphasis. Particularly interesting is the new technique of transposing the human figure into irregularly defined areas of dark and light which correspond to shadows on the body and replace even the clothing.

The Vienna Union of Arts and Crafts, founded in 1884, which had its premises in Vienna I, Schauflergasse 2, opened new rooms in 1912 in the Stalburggasse in order to be able to cater for the interests of native Austrian craftsmen. To this organization belonged the independent craftsmen, artist designers and those interested in promoting arts and crafts. The Union published at that time a magazine called *Monthly Notices of the Vienna Union of Arts and Crafts*.

122·8 × 90·4 cm

Colour lithography from artist's design.

Printed by J. Weiner, Vienna.

29

ERWIN PUCHINGER

Vienna Union of Arts and Crafts

1912

The textile ornamentation of this lottery advertisement with its text blocks is typical of lottery advertising in Austria around 1910. These posters usually had no picture and sought to give the impression of an official savings stamp, consisting of an often carpet-like ornamental pattern and a richly decorated border. The Imperial Arms of Austria invariably occurs—here we have it no less than nine times—in order to emphasize that this lottery is organized 'By explicit permission of His Royal, Imperial and Apostolic Majesty'. In this poster the coat of arms has the effect almost of a pattern.

The monopoly of lotteries in Austria is held by the State, in order to prevent misuse and to control gambling fever. As in the rest of Europe in the sixteenth century, in the smaller town and market lotteries, those round jars were used with necks so small that the tickets could not be seen by the man drawing the lots. In such lotteries, the prizes were mostly silver, porcelain or pictures. These jar lotteries were supplanted in the eighteenth century by number lotteries, which were introduced in 1751, and came under State control in 1787. In 1721 for the first time there had been a class lottery; in 1813 the State Lottery was legally regulated by the Lottery Patent (number lotteries, class lotteries, tombola etc.). From 1871 gambling was severely restricted. Although number lotteries were officially suppressed, they are still organized today, for fiscal reasons. The 'explicit permission' referred to on the posters emphasizes the special permission granted separately for each lottery. Other posters of a similar nature state that tickets can be bought 'at the Imperial Department of Lotteries, Vienna III, Vordere Zollamtstraβe 7, at all lottery offices, in lottery collection offices, tobacco kiosks, tax offices, post offices, railway and boat stations and all exchange offices'.

30
RUDOLF JUNK
Extraordinary State Lottery
1913

126×95 cm.

Colour zincography from the artist's design.

Print from the Imperial State Printing Works, Vienna.

ÜBER ALLERHÖCHSTE
ERMÄCHTIGUNG
SEINER KAISERLI
CHEN UND KÖNIG
LICHEN APOSTOLI
SCHEN MAJESTÄT

AUSSERORDENTLICHE K·K· STAATSLOTTERIE
FÜR GEMEINSAME MILITÄRWOHLTÄTIGKEITSZWECKE

 21.146 TREFFER IN BAREM GELDE IM GESAMTBETRAGE VON **625.000 KRONEN**

ZIEHUNG 3·JULI·1913  **EIN LOS 4 KRONEN**

 **HAUPTTREFFER**

200.000

 **KRONEN**
K·K·LOTTOGEFÄLLSDIREKTION·WIEN·III/2

RUDOLF JUNK INV. K·K·HOF- UND STAATSDRUCKEREI

A poster advertising the State Zoo in Budapest. If one reads the text and then looks up, it seems as if the lettering is continued upwards until suddenly one catches sight of the vulture who is seen only in outline and whose sole sign of life is one watchful eye. Moreover, this outline seems to cut a window in the poster. The negative and positive spaces are carefully balanced.

This poster announces that the Budapest Zoo possesses a Palm House, an Aquarium, a Film Theatre, a Café, a Restaurant and a Dairy. From 1 May a symphony concert will be held every afternoon and evening. The coat of arms of Budapest is incorporated in the text.

94 × 63·2 cm.

Colour lithography from artist's design.

Printed by the Budapest Printing Works.

31

MICHAEL BIRO

Allatkert

1914

This poster advertises a lottery held for charitable purposes. The effect of depth given by the overlapping and shortening of the numerous white surfaces is counteracted by the regularity of the colour surfaces, especially the lilac brown background. The upper part of the picture is skilfully linked with the text at the bottom by the papers and the bold lines of the yellow portion. An important point, too, is the lack of any colour for the body of Fortuna, who is sticking her tongue out at the spectator.

This dual-purpose lottery—every ticket could also be used as a postcard—was in the Austro-Hungarian tradition of lotteries which were publicized as being 'realistic, with cash prizes', and had been popular from very early days. A particularly piquant note is struck by the fact that the lottery, at that time considered immoral, was to be raised in moral status by the possibility of winning a work of art. On the other hand this poster does also indicate the interest already shown by large sections of the population in the arts.

186·5 × 95 cm.

Colour lithograph from artist's design, printed in two parts.

Printed by J. Weiner, Vienna.

32

JOSEF MARIA AUCHENTALLER
Postcard Lottery
1900

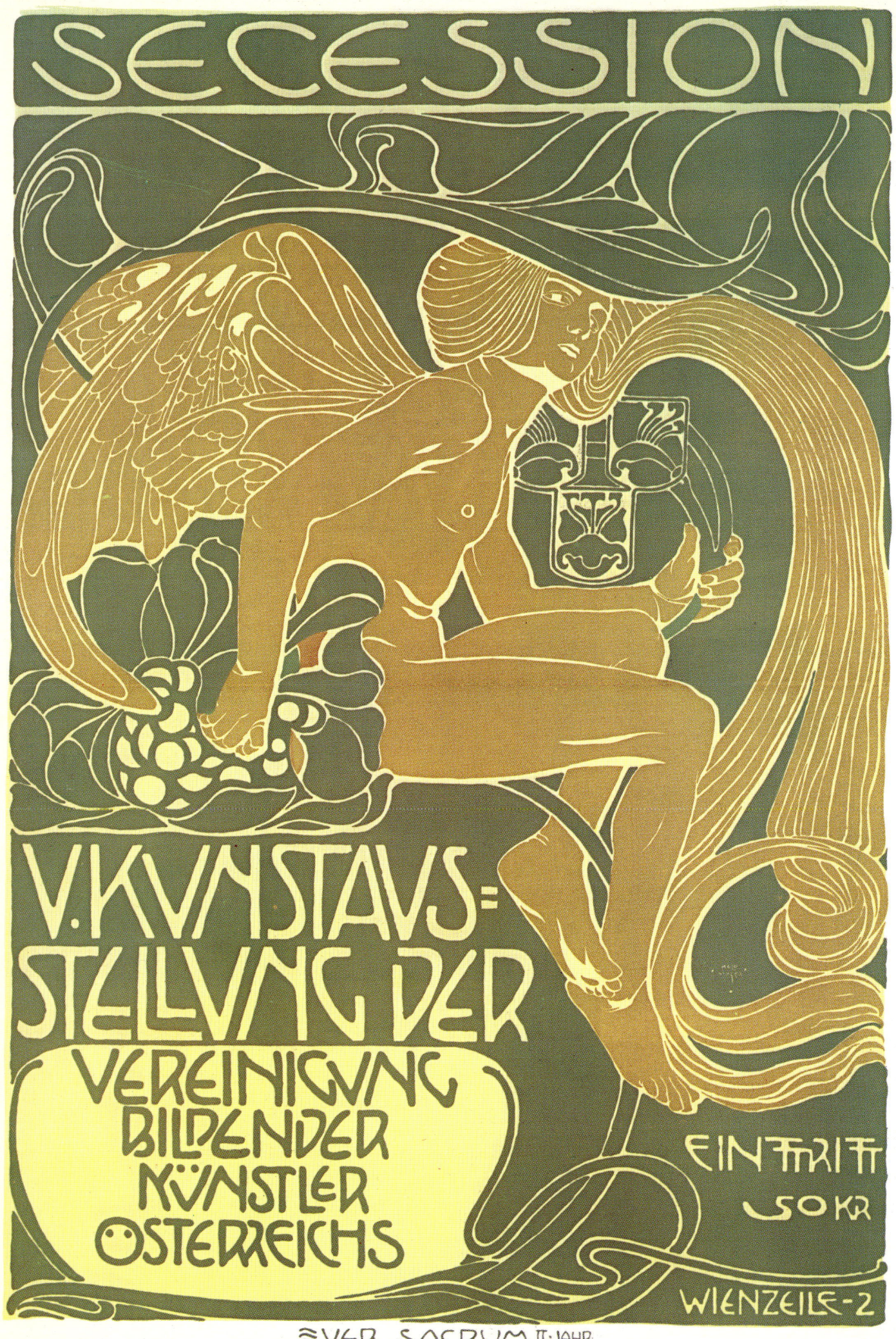

33

JULIUS KLINGER
Spring Show
1914
preceding pages

This poster for an art exhibition demonstrates the method emphasized strongly by the artist at that time of using advertising symbols in poster design. He was very much opposed to a purely artistic concept of poster design, which neglected the commercial aspect. A poster should be more than a picture and a corresponding text, since the symbolic representation of a product advertised it far more quickly and effectively than either word or picture alone. Klinger once wrote that the American flag was the best poster for the United States, since it was the most easily understood symbol of that country. On this poster Klinger symbolizes three things: Spring, and Arts and Crafts as modern ornamentation. This ornamentation is not an end in itself, but merely serves the advertising symbolism. Nevertheless it speaks highly for the artist that in spite of the inartistic purpose of the advertising symbolism, he manages to find such an eminently artistic solution.

The Hohenzollern House of Arts and Crafts, founded in 1879, originally H. Hirschwald G.m.b.H. and later Friedmann und Weber, was situated first in the Leipzigerstraße 13 and after about 1912 in the Königgrätzstraße 8. It sold furniture, carvings, materials and antique ornaments, and also organized numerous exhibitions of contemporary art. From other posters we learn that in 1909 there was an exhibition entitled 'The Lady in Art and Fashion', and that in 1910 an exhibition, 'Art and Commerce' (with posters) was organized by the German Hagen Museum of Art in Trade and Industry. In 1912 a Silhouette exhibition was held, incorporating a Gallery of Fashion. A prospectus informs us that between 1 October 1904 and 1 January 1905, the following exhibitions were to be held: 'An Exhibition of the Vienna Workshop, Professor Josef Hoffmann and Professor Koloman Moser. At the same time, a special exhibition of Ferdinand Andri's carvings, children's toys, grotesques; ceramics by Bruno Emmel; sculpture by Frau Luksch-Makovsky; sculpture in wood and porcelain by Richard Luksch; sculpture by Franz Metzner—Vienna.'

71·2 × 94·9 cm.

Colour lithography from artist's design.

Printed by Hollerbaum and Schmidt, Berlin.

34

KOLOMAN MOSER
Fifth Exhibition of
the *Secession*
1899
left

This is an art exhibition poster which better than any other represents the descriptive picture in European art at the turn of the century, in the symbolism, the floral lines of the drawing, the stylized simplification of an image of Nature, the similarity in shape of positive and negative surfaces, the script, so free in spite of the ornamentation, and the balance of figure and space in the picture. It shows a winged genius with the badge of the *Secession*, designed by Moser. Also noteworthy is the edge of the poster which appears like the edge of a net cast over the whole picture.

The fifth exhibition of the *Secession* was the first specialized exhibition of the Union, and was devoted exclusively to drawing and the graphic arts.

100 × 69·5 cm.

Colour lithography and gold-bronze dusting process from artist's design.

Printed by Albert Berger, Vienna.

Variations in format: 56 × 41 cm. The Albertina has no fewer than five colour variations of this poster.

V. Lithographic direct flat-bed machine at the turn of the century.

1. Carriage; 2. Eccentric disc with piston; 3. Ink grinding rollers, ink distribution rollers; 4. Ink distributor; 5. Ink-tray; 6. Stone; 7. Inking rollers; 8. Printing cylinder; 9. Supply of paper; 10. Damping rollers; 11. Tray.

Diagram adapted from Fig. 13 of Friedrich Hesse's book *La Chromolithographie*, Paris 1896.

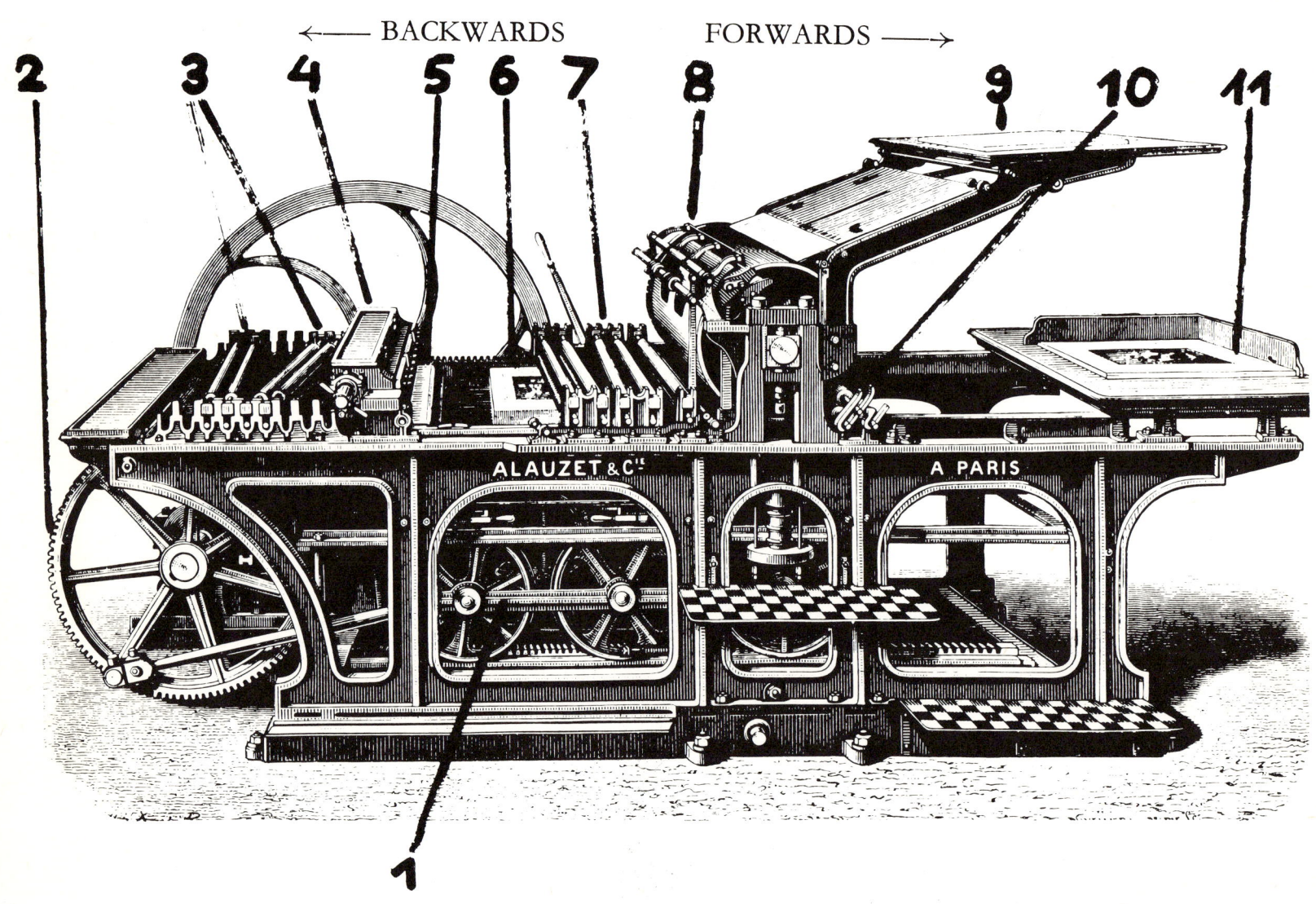

POSTER PRINTING TECHNIQUES

Owing to its close connection with commercial interests, poster designing is subject to laws other than those governing the hand-produced work of a graphic artist, where design and printing, idea and execution, are carried out by the same hand. Around the turn of the century it is really only from France that we find posters hand-lithographed by the artist. This is partly explained by the fact that Chéret, the great model for all poster artists, was a trained lithographer and personally drew all of his posters—over 1000 in all—on the stone. In England there were at that time hardly any hand-lithographed posters. The English looked at poster production from a purely commercial point of view and therefore excluded artists from printing works. They were allowed simply to make a coloured drawing of the size required for the poster, and this was transferred on to the stone by the lithographers. It is said that English printing works charged for printing 1000 copies of a poster in four or five colours, and including the artist's commission, only a quarter of the fee demanded in France by the artist for simply drawing the design on the stone.

In Austria there is another reason for the paucity of hand-produced posters: an artist was usually only permitted to draw on the stone if he could prove he had had training as a lithographer. The Union of Lithographers adhered very strictly to this regulation, which hindered for some time the development of the artistic poster. For many artists designed their posters in gouache or oils, and the lithographers tried to reproduce the thick, massy colour of this 'poster painting' in planographic printing. The artists were not at this stage transposing their ideas into a form suitable for the lithographic process; the lithographers of the old school used to imitate the colours of the painted design by an even distribution of dots, and this was responsible for the exaggeratedly smooth and over-decorated effect seen in many of the early posters. But when the lithographers designed their own posters they had frequent recourse to the pattern books for the reproduction of documents in the Renaissance style; Chéret's importance lay in the fact that he broke away from these formalistic designs and aimed at creating a sketch effect. With only a few colour plates he achieved his many colour nuances solely by means of overprinting his basic colours. Artists at first remained faithful to the old traditional allegories, which they endowed with new attributes. An early example is an engraving of Marco Pitteri by Giovanni Battista Piazzetta, who even in the eighteenth century was advertising on behalf of a Venetian silk manufacturer. In this poster a cherub with mulberry twigs, a female figure measuring the cloth and the god of fame were supposed to illustrate the inscription 'Fabrica di Panni di Seta d'Antonio Ferrari in Venetia'.

To limit the intervention of lithographers, photomechanical processes for the creation of posters were introduced at an early date. Various posters by Eugène Grasset which are considered by many to be ordinary colour lithography were actually manufactured by designing them on zinc plates, printing them by the letterpress process and then colouring by stencil. This method was also cheaper. One of the cleverest examples in this field is Franz von Stuck's poster for the International Exhibition of Art in Munich in 1897, which shows a head and shoulders of Pallas Athena. An enlarged print of the original was copied on to a sensitized stone and after being etched was used as the plate for a colour lithograph.

The developments in this field in England are particularly noteworthy. Since the artists were not allowed in the printing works, they soon changed to making large-scale designs which were less liable to be spoiled by the lithographer. Naturally, the printers also saved a good deal of money, since they used so few colour plates, and they also did not need to etch them so painstakingly. At the same time a technique was being developed in France and Germany aimed at increasing the light tones of a lithograph with scrapers or etching needles; Adolf von Menzel made masterly use of this technique in his experiments with brush and scraper on stone (1851). The process was combined with the splatter technique, used by Henri de Toulouse-Lautrec in posters with such unparalleled success.

Poster lithography developed late in Vienna, a fact attributable partly to the relatively unimportant position held by lithography there, as compared with that of the highly-developed book-printing industry. Very little is known about its early period. In 1816 the University printer, Karl Gerold, had sent in a petition for permission to set up his own lithographic press, and Aloys Senefelder himself had come to Vienna to assist in setting it up, but we hear little about its subsequent activities. An Institute of Lithography was founded which reached a high standard of efficiency. In spite of this, planographic printing developed very slowly in Vienna, unlike neighbouring Bavaria. It was not until 1846, when the Lithographic Works was amalgamated with the State Printing Works and Alois Auer turned his attention to this branch of printing, that a tremendous development took place. In this one institute the number of lithographic presses rose from seven to 40, and in the years between 1845 and 1850 the technical staff in this department increased from 21 to 109. In 1882 this institute already possessed three direct flat-bed machines and still used fifteen hand presses. At the same time the Vienna book-printing industry was taking as its model the equipment of the Institute for Military Geography, which always purchased the very latest innovations and which, together with the Austrian army, played an important part in the development of printing techniques in the field of cartography.

To the leading role of book-publishing in Vienna we must add the fact that originally the woodcut was preferred to lithography. Naturally, the development of lithography was further hindered by the fact that the expensive materials had to be obtained from abroad—stone from Bavaria, dyes and rollers from France. A considerable improvement was made by the alteration of the Craft Regulations in 1877, when the various craft groups in the printing industry were united under one banner, The Association of Book, Lithographic and Copperplate Printers. At that time there were in Vienna 73 book-printers and xylographers, with approximately 1750 assistants and apprentices, as opposed to 83 lithographers and owners of lithographic presses, with roughly 900 assistants and apprentices. Quite imposing technical successes were achieved with the posters printed by Eduard Sieger and designed by Franz Gerasch. These posters are up to eight feet long and five feet wide and were printed in one lithographic process on zinc plates.

PRINTING TECHNIQUES

Lithographic stones were not only expensive, they were also very fragile. The largest stones did not exceed 120×160 cm. and weighed 400–500 kg. In 1854—prior to the enlargement of the Lithographic Department in the State Printing Works under Auer—the stone store contained 3200 stones, from which annually about 400,000 sheets (formulae, documents, lithographic and chromolithographic illustrations to the works of the various subordinate bureaux of the ministries) were printed. However, such a number can be misleading. For example, the 300 plates of the four volume work *Masterpieces of Industrial Art & Sculpture at the International Exhibition of 1862*, London 1863, would have required 3000 stones, a fact which is stated in the foreword of the work. Such figures help us to understand the constant attempts to print lithographically not from stones but from zinc and aluminium plates (zincography and algraphy).

Lithography is based on the principle of the antagonism between water and grease. The limestone blocks, which are ground to absolute smoothness, are of a very fine texture; without doubt the best quality of stone is quarried in Bavaria at Solnhofen. Greasy litho-inks, crayons or chalks penetrate some way into the porous stone, so that after the surface has been washed, when it is run over with a roller, the greasy outlines of the drawing, which reject the water, are covered with printing-ink and accept it. The wet portions, which have not been greased, reject the ink. However, in order to fix the greasy drawing more securely and to make the non-greasy parts more able to repel the dye, another process is required, called etching. This etching liquid, which consists of water, gum arabic and nitric acid, is brushed on evenly over the whole surface until it has been absorbed. Without the gum arabic the acid would etch the stone too strongly and thus spoil the sharpness of the outline. The liquid is then washed off with turpentine and water, so that the drawing almost disappears. The greasy substance, affected by the acid, has penetrated the stone (the carbonic acid in the limestone has become fatty acid). The non-greasy surfaces have also undergone a chemical change due to the etching (the carbonic acid becomes nitric acid in the limestone). These surfaces have become extremely water-absorbent, and repel all grease. If the stone dries during the colouring process, colour will also settle on the non-greasy surfaces, but if these surfaces are dampened once more, this is taken off again when the roller passes over them. Following this etching and the subsequent inking with the roller, the stone is now ready for printing. In the press the colour, with the paper laid on the stone, is removed by means of a scraper.

The treatment of zinc and aluminium plates is similar in principle. A brief explanation of lithographic colour printing might help the reader. Only one colour can be printed from a stone; therefore for each colour another stone is needed. But there must always be a main contour- or key-stone, on which every detail of the picture is drawn. In chromolithography every change of colour must be traced as a fine line on this contour-stone. Then the tracing is transferred to as many other stones as there are colours to be printed. Each of these colour stones is then prepared with those details which are to be printed from it, all the other lines transferred from the contour-stone being removed before the etching takes place. When the colours are being superimposed on the print, care must be taken with glazing colour to print in a certain sequence; for example, to produce green, first the yellow and then the blue is printed. If the reverse were done, the yellow would extinguish the blue.

In order to describe the difference between the expensive chromo-posters, which were usually destined to be preserved, and the zincographic posters printed with a few colours only, for everyday use, distinction was made at the turn of the century between posters and advertisements; for an advertisement, bright colours were essential to achieve rapid impressions in the viewer, whereas the posters, like paintings, were intended to make a lasting impression on the public over a considerable period. Zincography was generally used for cheaper prints, whereas algraphy, invented by Joseph Scholz at Mainz in 1892, made possible prints of very high quality. The specialist teacher Karl Kampmann brought algraphy to the Vienna Teaching and Experimental Institute of Graphic Art in 1896; shortly afterwards it was introduced to the Institute of Military Geography and the State Printing Works, and was being taught at the School of Arts and Crafts in drawing classes by Felician von Myrbach, who always executed his illustrations in the most modern techniques. Even before Scholz, whose process came into general use, John Mullaby and Lothrop L. Bullock are said to have printed from aluminium plates. Zinc and aluminium later made possible the adaptation of lithographic presses to the rotation principle. In the lithographic flat-bed machines which were generally employed in Vienna by the turn of the century for printing posters, the mechanical means of pressing the paper against the stone was a cylinder instead of a scraper. Whereas 50 prints an hour could be made with a hand press, the direct flat-bed machine could produce up to 500 prints, and its speed of output was governed only by the efficiency of the assistant removing and replacing the paper. Later, this was done by mechanical means, which considerably increased the speed of production.

How does such a direct flat-bed machine work? On to the main framework are screwed the carriage for the bed (1), and the sides where the cylinder and the dampening- and inking-rollers are housed. The stone (6) lies on the bed and can be adjusted to the correct height for printing according to its thickness. The bed also holds the inking-tray (5). By means of the eccentric disc and the piston (2), the flat-bed, stone and inking-tray are pushed backwards and forwards in the framework. When the bed moves backwards, the ink tray (5), which was under the inking rollers, is set in motion, and passes under the ink-distributor (4) to the grinding-rollers, which spread the ink evenly on the tray. At the same time the stone, which on the forward motion of the bed had delivered the paper to the printing-cylinder (8) and had passed under the dampening-roller (10,) passes under it once more on the return movement, goes under the printing-cylinder without contact and comes to the inking-rollers (7) where it receives fresh ink. When the carriage moves forward once more, the stone comes under the printing-rollers and the print is made; the inking-tray (5) is brought by this movement under the inking-rollers (7) and transfers to them the colour applied to it by the ink-distributor. Each time an apprentice must place one sheet of paper from the supply (9) on the printing-cylinder and take the

PRINTING TECHNIQUES

printed sheet from the stone, putting it on the tray (11).

In order to strengthen the stone and the printing machinery—for the mechanical wear and tear caused by this process is considerable—the stones were strongly etched; from such a stone, even very large editions could be printed with perfect reproduction. Such strong etching was particularly popular when transfers were made. In this process the artists did not draw upon the stone, but on a special transfer paper, and this drawing was then transferred to a stone in a printing works. For this strong etching, the burning and etching process invented by Josef Eberle was found to be most effective. Resin is laid over the drawing and burned in by means of a flame. This has the effect of toughening the drawing and allowing the stone to be etched more strongly.

Bronze colours were not printed lithographically but were dusted on. For this purpose these surfaces were lithographically suppressed by means of a suppressing colour which had been mixed with a particularly sticky varnish. Ochre was the usual base for gold-bronze, a silvery-grey shade for silver or aluminium bronze, so that in the event of the bronze surface being damaged, the related colour beneath it would preserve the total effect. The bronze dust was then applied to the sticky undercoat either with a gentle pressure on a brush covered with flannel or cotton, or else dusted on mechanically by a bronzing machine. The superfluous dust was carefully blown off.

We must mention as well offset printing, also known as transfer printing. In this, a rubber cylinder transfers the lithographic print from the original plate to the paper. The advantage of this technique is that even the coarsest paper can be printed cleanly and clearly, and the plates are more resistant to wear and tear. As early as the turn of the century this process (algraphy or zincography) enabled the rotational printing of paper straight from the web.

In conclusion, here are a few details about the format and number of these posters. The sizes are based on the combination or division of the normal paper size (which in Vienna was 95 × 63·5 cm.). There were very few variations from this norm, because the advertising agencies had naturally based their charges on them and either refused, or charged extra for, posters deviating from them. On the other hand the advertising agencies were partly responsible for determining the size of the edition, because they always quoted for certain definite quantities of posters displayed. The Viennese advertising agencies at the turn of the century only possessed 600 advertising hoardings or pillars, and this restricted the number of posters printed. In Vienna no extra editions without the text were printed either for artists or the poster trade, as was common in Paris at that time.

CHRONOLOGICAL TABLE OF EVENTS IN THE VIENNA ART WORLD AT THE TURN OF THE CENTURY

1886–1900 Gustav Klimt paints the ceilings of the Burgtheater

1894 4 September: Gustav Klimt and Franz Match are commissioned to paint the Faculty pictures. In this year which marked the twenty-fifth anniversary of the *Künstlerhaus*, exhibitions of the Munich *Secession* and the Artists of Düsseldorf opened on 1 December

1894–1900 Otto Wagner builds the city railway

1894–1898 Otto Wagner builds the Nadelwehr Nussdorf (Regulation of the Danube Canal)

1895 May: The Seven Club founded

Publication of Otto Wagner's *Moderne Architektur*

1895–1900 Publication of *Allegories, New Series* (with designs by Gustav Klimt, Koloman Moser, Carl Otto Czeschka and others)

1896 Vienna Congress Exhibition in the Imperial Austrian Museum of Art and Industry (the last great attempt of this museum to imbue contemporary arts and crafts with the concepts of historicism)

1897 3 April: Founding of the Union of Creative Artists of Austria

24 May: Resignation of the Union from the Association of Creative Artists of Vienna (*Künstlerhaus*)

3 August: Arthur von Scala becomes Director of the Imperial Museum of Art and Industry

1897–1900 Publication of Adolf Loos' *Spoken into the Void*

1898 25 March: First exhibition of the Union of Creative Artists of Austria (*Secession*), in the premises of the Gartenbaugesellschaft (Gardeners' Association)

19 April: Jubilee Exhibition of the *Künstlerhaus* in conjunction with the Musicians' Guild as a tribute to the Emperor Franz Josef on the fiftieth anniversary of his accession. (Works by Max Klinger, Arnold Böcklin, Adolph von Menzel, Giovanni Segantini, Walter Crane, William Morris, Albert Besnard, Pierre Puvis de Chavannes, Claude Monet, Auguste Rodin and others)

2 August: Archduke Rainer dismissed as patron of the Imperial Museum of Art and Industry

12 November: New constitution for the Austrian Museum; William Unger and Otto Wagner members of the Committee

Otto Wagner builds the Majolika houses

Publication of first volume of the periodical *Ver Sacrum*

Publication of periodical *Kunst und Kunsthandwerk* (Art and Arts and Crafts)

Publication of annual folio of Society for the Duplicating Art

1899 16 February: In the first session of the Art Council, Carl Moll demands an 'Austrian Gallery of Modern Art'

25 February: Felician von Myrbach becomes provisional head of the School of Arts and Crafts

April: Josef Hoffmann joins the staff of the School of Arts and Crafts

Summer: Joseph Maria Olbrich is called to Darmstadt

27 September: An exhibition of Japanese coloured woodcuts opens in the Imperial Museum of Art and Industry

Adolf Loos decorates the Café Museum

1899–1900 Max Fabiani builds the premises of the firm of Portois & Fix at Vienna III, Ungargasse

1899–1907 Third period of building for the new Hofburg under Friedrich Ohmann, and the setting up of a programme for sculptures

Publication of Rudolf von Larisch's *Uber Zeitschriften im Dienste der Kunst* (On periodicals in the service of art), Munich 1899

1900 29 January: Foundation of the *Hagenbund*

January: Sixth exhibition of the *Secession*: Japanese Art

March: Seventh exhibition of the *Secession*: Gustav Klimt's *Philosophy* is exhibited

12 March: Felician von Myrbach is named as Director of the Museum of Art and Industry

14 April: In the 1900 World Exhibition in Paris, a Viennese Room is shown

July: Koloman Moser is appointed to the staff of the School of Arts and Crafts

Eighth exhibition of the *Secession*: Works of Charles Robert Ashbee and the Mackintosh Group

29 November: The *Hagenbund* resigns from the *Künstlerhaus*

31 December: Walter Crane Exhibition in the Imperial Museum of Art and Industry

Publication of periodical *Das Interieur* (Editor Joseph August Lux)

Publication of Hermann Bahr's *Secession* (Buchhandlung Rosner)

Publication of *Die Quelle* (The Source), vol. 1 (Martin Gerlach Vienna 1900)

1901 24 February: Exhibition of works of Hokusai in the Imperial Austrian Museum of Art and Industry

March: Tenth exhibition of the *Secession*: Gustav Klimt's *Medecine* is shown

Spring: Alfred Roller joins the staff of the School of Arts and Crafts

7 June: The directors of the *Künstlerhaus* present a petition to the Minister concerning the setting up of a Gallery of Modern Art in Vienna. The *Secession* had refused to support this move and had sent its own memorandum

November: Twelfth exhibition of the *Secession*: Jan Toorop and various collections of Swedish, Norwegian, Finnish, Swiss and Russian artists

1902 January: First exhibition of the *Hagenbund* in their own premises at the Zedlitzgasse 6

17 January to 19 March: Emil Orlik holds a series of lectures in the Museum of Art and Industry on 'Japanese Life and Art'

February: Thirteenth exhibition of the *Secession*: among other items shown were a number of works by the Munich Union of Artists, Die Scholle (Native Earth)

April: Fourteenth exhibition of the *Secession*: Klinger's *Beethoven*

November: Fifteenth exhibition of the *Secession*: among other exhibitors were the Union of Polish Artists (Sztuka) and Vienna Art in the Home

2 November: The *Jungbund*, founded in this year, exhibits for the first time at the Autumn Exhibition of the *Künstlerhaus*

Rudolf von Larisch is engaged to teach at the School of Arts and Crafts

Carl Otto Czeschka is engaged as assistant drawing master at the School of Arts and Crafts

1903 January: Sixteenth exhibition of the *Secession*: The Development of Impressionism in Painting and Sculpture

May: The Vienna Workshop is founded in two rooms at Heumühlgasse 4

June: The Vienna Workshop is constituted as 'Vienna Workshop Production Company of Art Craftsmen in Vienna'

1 September: Franz Metzner is taken on the staff of the School of Arts and Crafts

October: Vienna Workshop moves to Neustiftgasse 32

November: Eighteenth exhibition of the *Secession*: Collection of works by Gustav Klimt

The State Gallery of Modern Art is founded

1903–1905 Josef Plecnik builds the Haus Zacherl at Vienna I, Brandstätte

Publication of Adolf Loos' *Das Andere,* Vienna 1903

1904 Beginning of the year: Rejection of the suggestion of the *Secession* on the occasion of the World Exhibition at St. Louis that Gustav Klimt's Faculty pictures should be shown in a representative room designed by Josef Hoffmann

January: Nineteenth exhibition of the *Secession*: Works by Ferdinand Hodler, Edvard Munch and Jan Thorn Prikker

December: Aubrey Beardsley exhibition at the Miethke Gallery, Dorotheergasse

1904–1906 Otto Wagner builds the Post Office Savings Building

1904–1906 Otto Wagner builds the Purkersdorf Sanatorium

1904–1907 Otto Wagner builds the church at the Steinhof

Publication of the periodical *Hohe Warte* (The lookout tower) by Joseph August Lux

Publication of the periodical *Der liebe Augustin*

Publication of Rudolf von Larisch's *Uber Leserlichkeit von ornamentalen Schriften* (On the Legibility of ornamental script), Vienna 1904.

1905 January: Twenty-seventh exhibition of the *Secession*: European Plastic Arts

February: The Miethke Gallery, after a change of ownership, negotiated with the *Secession* on the subject of acting as a sales gallery for the movement. These negotiations broke down, and the firm opened new premises with an exhibition of the Vienna Workshop and artists closely associated with them (Carl Otto Czeschka and others)

10 March: The Art Commission of the University rejects the provisional installation of Gustav Klimt's *Faculty Pictures*

20 April: Felician von Myrbach, after a series of unfortunate circumstances, is granted a pension

June: The Klimt Group leaves the *Secession*

November: Seventeenth exhibition of the *Hagenbund*. A collection from the *Jungbund* and other works

Michael Powolny and Berthold Löffler found the workshops Vienna Ceramics, whose works are banned from the Vienna Workshop

1905–1911 Josef Hoffmann, the Vienna Workshop and Gustav Klimt create the Palais Stoclet in Brussels

Publication of Rudolf von Larisch's *Unterricht in ornamentaler Schrift* (Course on ornamental script)

1906 January: Twenty-fifth exhibition of the *Secession*: Union of Artists Die Scholle (Native Earth), with woodcuts by Wassily Kandinsky

5 October: Opening of the theatre cabaret Hölle (Hell) in the cellar of the Theatre on the Vienna River. It was designed by Heinrich Lefler and Ludwig Ferdinand Graf, members of the *Hagenbund*

Franz Cižek joins the staff of the School of Arts and Crafts

1907 January: Twenty-eighth exhibition of the *Secession*: The Munich *Secession*

July: Exhibition of Gustav Klimt's finished *Faculty Pictures* at the Miethke Gallery

October: The cabaret of the Vienna Workshop, Fledermaus, is opened at 33 Kärntnerstraße

1 October: Carl Otto Czeschka is called to Hamburg, but collaborates until 1913 with the Vienna Workshop

Autumn: Koloman Moser resigns from the Committee of the Vienna Workshop

November: The Vienna Workshop opens a sales office at Am

Graben 15

Adolf Loos builds the Kärntner Bar, Vienna I, Kärntner Durchgang

1908 The Diamond Jubilee of Emperor Franz Josef I has a stimulating effect on art in Vienna

Beginning of the year: The Ministry of Education gives the Klimt group 30,000 crowns as a grant for an exhibition

21 March: Austrian Jubilee Art Exhibition in the *Künstlerhaus* in honour of the Diamond Jubilee of Franz Josef I.

3 April (on the eleventh anniversary of its foundation): Thirtieth exhibition of the *Secession,* dedicated to Franz Josef

18 May: the Eighth International Congress of Architects is opened in the Council Chamber of the House of Deputies

19 May: An International Exhibition of Building Art is opened at the Gardeners' Association

Exhibition in honour of the Emperor by the *Hagenbund* in conjunction with the Union of Polish Artists, Sztuka, and the Union of Creative Artists, Manes

End of May: Opening of the Arts Review

12 June: Exhibition in honour of the Emperor with historical tableaux from Austrian history. Architecture by Joseph Urban, groups and decorations by Heinrich Lefler, Berthold Löffler, Karl Hollitzer and Remigius Geyling

8 August: Death of Joseph Maria Olbrich in Düsseldorf; Archduke Ernst Ludwig von Hesse requests Gustav Klimt to come to Darmstadt as Olbrich's successor. Klimt suggests Josef Hoffmann, who declines

October: Thirty-first exhibition of the *Secession*: Modern Russian Art

Gardeners' Association exhibition in honour of the Jubilee: Our Emperor

November: Jubilee Art Exhibition of the Albrecht Dürer Association, Mariahilferstrasse 89A

6 December: First exhibition of the Osterreichischer Künstlerbund (Union of Austrian Artists) in the rooms of the Austrian Art Association, Vienna I, Weihburggasse

1908-1913 Otto Wagner builds the Lupus Clinic

Publication of Oskar Kokoschka's *Die träumenden Knaben* (The dreaming boys), Vienna 1908

1909 March: Retirement of Arthur von Scala, Director of the Imperial Museum of Art and Industry

1 May: Berthold Löffler becomes a permanent member of the staff of the School of Arts and Crafts

May: Sales office of Vienna Workshop opened in Karlsbad

12 June: Alfred Roller made head of the School of Arts and Crafts

Summer: International Art Show

October: Twenty-fourth exhibition of the *Secession*: Collection of works by Josef Engelhart

October: Thirtieth exhibition of the *Hagenbund*: Wilhelm Busch

End of 1909: Michael Powolny, Otto Prutscher and Oskar Strnad join the staff of the School of Arts and Crafts.

Egon Schiele, Albert Paris Gütersloh and others found the Neukunstgruppe (New Art Group)

1910 January: Exhibition of the Union of Hungarian Artists (Kéve) in the *Hagenbund*

7 May: International Exhibition of Hunting with an Art Pavilion: Collection of works by the Klimt group, the *Künstlerhaus* and the *Secession*

Autumn: Exhibition of Swedish artists in the *Hagenbund*

Adolf Loos builds the Steiner House, Vienna III, St. Veit-Gasse

1910-1911 Adolf Loos builds the house on the Michaelerplatz

1911 February: Special exhibition of the *Hagenbund,* with works by Otto Kokoschka, Albert Paris Gütersloh, Anton Faistauer and others

Miethke Gallery opens the new Arts Review, which had degenerated into a series of collections, with a Gustav Klimt Exhibition

Austrian pavilion at the International Art Exhibition in Rome

1912 January: Exhibition of Norwegian artists in the *Hagenbund*

January: Fortieth exhibition of the *Secession*: Posters

Spring: Thirty-eighth exhibition of the *Hagenbund*; last exhibition at the Exhibition Rooms in the Zedlitzgasse, the use of which was forbidden by the Viennese Civic Authorities

Foundation of the Austrian Society for the Promotion of the Creative Arts by Josef Hoffmann and the Vienna Workshop

Amalgamation of the Vienna Ceramics with the workshops of Franz Schleiss, the new company being called Vereinigte Viener und Gmunder Keramik (United Vienna and Gmund Ceramics)

1913 Fritz Waerndorfer leaves the Vienna Workshop and goes to America. A businessman named Kurz becomes new manager. The Primavesi family finance the workshops. The artists' workshop *Wiener Werkstätte* is founded

International Black and White Exhibition of the Academic Society for Literature and Music

1913-1914 Josef Hoffmann builds the Primavesi House, Vienna XIII, Gloriettegasse

1914 Beginning of the year: the Miethke Gallery shows an exhibition of works by Pablo Picasso

Exhibition of the Union of Austrian Artists in Rome

Oskar Kokoschka paints *Die Windbraut* (Bride of the wind)

Josef Hoffmann builds the pavilion at the exhibition of the Society for the Promotion of the Creative Arts in Cologne

THE ARTISTS

Ferdinand Andri, 10.3.1871 Waidhofen/Ybbs—19.5.1956 Vienna.
Pupil of Berger and Lichtenfels at the Vienna Academy. In 1892 he continued his studies in Karlsruhe. 1899-1909 member of the *Secession,* 1905 President of the *Secession.*

Josef Maria Auchentaller, 2.8.1865 Vienna—31.12.1949 Grado.
Pupil of Rumpler at the Vienna Academy. 1893-1895 Professor in Munich. Member of the *Secession* from 1898. Moved to Grado in 1901.

J. Beran—probably the same person as Lajos Beran. 9.6.1882 Budapest—5.1.1943 Budapest. Pupil of Ede Telcs in Budapest, studied at the Vienna Academy.

Mihaly (Michael) Biro, 30.11.1886 Budapest—30.11.1948 Budapest.
Studied in Budapest, Paris and London. After 1919 he emigrated to Vienna and later to America. He returned to Budapest in 1945.

Leopold Burger, 9.10.1861 Vienna—11.11.1903 Brixen.
Studied at the Vienna Academy and also under the theatrical painter Fux. Member of the *Künstlerhaus* from 1891, and of the *Hagenbund* from 1900.

Ernst Deutsch, 3.8.1883 Vienna —?
Pupil of the Vienna School of Arts and Crafts and of Gustav Klimt. Moved to Berlin in 1911.

Leopold Forstner, 2.11.1878 Leonfelden Upper Austria—5.11.1936 Stockerau.
Pupil at the Vienna School of Arts and Crafts under Karger and Moser and of the Munich Academy under Herterich. In 1906 he founded the Vienna Mosaic Workshops.

Remigius Geyling, 29.6.1878 Vienna—living in Vienna.
Studied under Karger at the Vienna School of Arts and Crafts from 1911-1913 and from 1922-1945 Stage Manager at the Vienna Burgtheater, 1913-1922 Director of the Society for Film Art.

Arnošt Hofbauer, 26.4.1869 Prague—11.1.1944 Prague.
Pupil of Zeniska at the Prague School of Arts and Crafts and of Pirnera and Hynaise at the Prague Academy, member of the Manes Artists' Union Wrote, among other works, a treatise on Japanese art in 1908.

Josef Hoffmann, 15.12.1870 Pirnitz/Moravia—7.5.1956 Vienna.
Studied under Hasenauer and Wagner at the Vienna Academy. From 1899 Professor at the Vienna School of Arts and Crafts. Member of the Seven Club, from 1896 member of the *Künstlerhaus,* from 1897 member of the *Secession.* Co-founder of the Vienna Workshops. Member of the Klimt Group, co-organiser of the Arts Review, founder of the Austrian Society for the Promotion of the Creative Arts.

Rudolf Junk, 23.2.1880 Vienna—20.12.1943 Vienna.
Student at Vienna University, where he studied German and Celtic languages. In 1903 he became a D.Phil.; he studied under Lefler at the Vienna Academy, was a member of the *Hagenbund* from 1904, and of the *Künstlerhaus* from 1924.

Adolf Karpellus, 8.1.1896 Neu-Sandec/Galicia—18.12.1919 Vienna.
Pupil of Griepenkerl and Trenkwald at the Vienna Academy, then studied at the Academie Julian in Paris. Member of the Seven Club, member of the *Künstlerhaus* from 1905 (an exhibition of his works was held there in 1905).

Gustav Klimt, 14.7.1862 Vienna—6.2.1918 Vienna.
As a student of the School of Arts and Crafts at Vienna he had as teachers Laufberger, Rieser, Minnigerode, Hrachowna and Berger. He shared a studio with Ernst Klimt and Franz Matsch. Member of the *Künstlerhaus* from 1891. Co-founder and first president of the *Secession* 1897. 1905 left the *Secession* and formed the Klimt Group. Collaborated with the Vienna Workshops. President of the Arts Review.

Julius Klinger, 22.5.1876 Vienna —?
Studied at the Vienna Technological School of Crafts, entered the drawing office of the *Wiener Mode* (Vienna Fashion), afterwards collaborated in the production of the *Meggendorfer Papers*. In 1897 he moved to Berlin, although he visited Vienna frequently in the following years. In Berlin and later during the twenties in Vienna once more, he was Director of the Poster Schools.

Oskar Kokoschka, 1.3.1886 Pöchlarn/Lower Austria—living in Villeneuve, Switzerland.
Pupil at the Vienna School of Arts and Crafts, where he studied under Czeschka and Löffler, he later collaborated in the Vienna Workshop, and also in the production of the *Sturm*. From 1920–1924 he was Professor at the Dresden Academy. From 1924–1934 he travelled, 1934–1938 he spent in Prague, then lived in London from that date until 1953.

František Kysela, 4.9.1881 Kourim—20.2.1941 Prague.
He studied at the Prague School of Arts and Crafts and at the Prague Academy under Schwaiger. From 1913 he was a teacher, from 1917 a Professor at the School of Arts and Crafts. Member of the artists' associations Manes and Skupina (founded 1911). Co-founder of the Czech Society for the Promotion of the Creative Arts.

Heinrich Lefler, 7.11.1863 Vienna—14.3.1919 Vienna.
Pupil of Griepenkerl at the Vienna Academy and also studied at the Munich Academy. From 1891 member of the *Künstlerhaus,* in 1900 co-founder of the *Hagenbund*.

Berthold Löffler (also Bertold), 28.9.1874 Nieder-Rosental/Bohemia —23.3.1960 Vienna.
Studied at the Vienna School of Arts and Crafts under Moser and Matsch. In 1905 he founded, together with Michael Powolny, the workshop Vienna Ceramics. In 1907 he took over Czeschka's class at the School of Arts and Crafts. Member of the *Künstlerhaus* from 1921.

Koloman Moser, 30.3.1868 Vienna—18.10.1918 Vienna.
Studied under Rumpler, Griepenkerl and Trenkwald at the Vienna Academy, and at the Vienna School of Arts and Crafts under Matsch. Member of the Seven Club, from 1896 member of the *Künstlerhaus,* in 1897 founding member of the *Secession*. In 1899 he became a teacher, in 1900 a Professor at the Vienna School of Arts and Crafts, in 1903 he was co-founder of the Vienna Workshop. Member of the Klimt group 1905. In 1907 he resigned from the Committee of the Vienna Workshop.

Joseph Maria Olbrich, 22.12.1867 Troppau—8.8.1908 Düsseldorf.
Studied under Hasenauer and Wagner at the Vienna Academy, was from 1894 a member of the *Künstlerhaus*; founder member of the *Secession,* whose exhibition rooms he built in 1898. In 1899 he was called to Darmstadt.

Emil Pirchan, 27.5.1884 Brno—20.12.1957 Vienna.
Studied at the Technical University in Vienna and at the Vienna Academy under Wagner. In 1914 he founded a poster school in Munich, in 1919 one in Berlin. In 1932 Artistic Stage Manager at the German Theatre in Prague. In 1936 he became Professor at the Vienna Academy. Member of the *Künstlerhaus* from 1943.

Ferdinand Pamberger.
Lithographer in Vienna. Frequently called on by Erwin Puchinger.

Erwin Puchinger, 31.7.1876 Vienna—17.6.1944 Vienna.
Pupil of the Viennese Schild Painting School and at the evening classes of the Teaching and Experimental Institute of Graphic Art. Studied also at the Vienna School of Arts and Crafts. From 1901 teacher at the Institute of Graphic Art. Member of the *Künstlerhaus* from 1912.

Hans Schliessmann, 6.2.1852 Mainz—14.2.1920 Vienna.
In 1866 attached to Xylographic Institute R. von Waldheim; later worked for numerous Vienna comic papers.

Victor Schufinsky, 28.7.1876 Vienna—7.10.1947 Vienna.
Studied at the Vienna School of Arts and Crafts under Myrbach. 1903–1905 assistant at the Teaching and Experimental Institute of Graphic Art; 1905–1915 teacher at the Technical School in Znaim. From 1918 he taught at the Vienna School of Arts and Crafts.

Imre (Emmerich) Simay, 16.12.1874 Budapest—19.4.1955 Erd.
Studied in Vienna and Munich under H. Zügel. His main sphere of interest was sculpture.

Leopold Stolba, 11.11.1863 Vienna—17.11.1929 Vienna.
Studied under Kundmann and Hellmer at the Academy; from 1900 member of the *Secession*.

POSTER EXHIBITIONS 1884-1914

The development of poster art was promoted by countless competitions. The great public interest in this new 'art of the street' can best be illustrated by a list of the poster exhibitions which to the knowledge of the author took place up to the year 1914. As far as possible places of exhibition are named; the brackets refer to the organizers.

1884 Brussels
Paris, Théâtre of the Passage Vivienne
Paris (Exhibition of American Posters)

1889 Nantes, Galerie Préaubert
Paris, Théâtre d'Apollon
Paris, Galerie du Théâtre d'Application
Paris, Palais des arts libéraux, Champ de Mars

1890 Bordeaux, Appel Printing Works
Nancy, Galerie Poirel

1891 Paris, Palais des Beaux-Arts, Champ de Mars

1892 Paris, Galerie M. Bodinier (Sagot)

1894 Leeds, City Art Gallery
London, Royal Aquarium
Milan
Paris, Palais de l'Industrie

1895 Chicago (*Century* and *Echo* poster show)
Chicago (*The Chicago Evening Post*)
London (Knight and Warren)
Massachusetts (Massachusetts Charitable Mechanic Association)
Milwaukee, Ethical Building
New York, Pratt Institute

1895 New York, Union League Club
New York, Wunderlich Gallery
Paris, Galerie Rapp, Champ de Mars
Rhode Island, Rhode Island School of Design
Rouen, Palais des Consuls

1896 Agen
Avesnes
Berlin, Museum of Arts and Crafts
Brussels, Maison d'Art
Dresden, Department of Prints and Drawings
Hamburg, Museum of Arts and Crafts
Liège
London, Royal Aquarium
Munich
New York, Grolier-Club
Reims
Richmond, Old Dominion Hospital
Rouen
St. Petersburg
Toulouse
Vienna, *Künstlerhaus*

1897 Aix la Chapelle, Suermondt-Museum
Düsseldorf
Kristiania, Art Club
New York (Hare & Co.)
Paris, Salon des Cents

1898 Berlin, Leipzigerstraße 128

1899 Chemnitz
Leipzig, Reichshof

1900 London, Crystal Palace

1901 London, Crystal Palace

1902 Düsseldorf
Turin, International Exhibition

1903 Gorlitz, Oberlausitz Society for Arts and Crafts

1905 Brno, Moravian Museum of Crafts

1906 Berlin, Künstlerhaus
Vienna, (Society for the Graphic Arts)

1907 Cologne, Museum of Arts and Crafts

1908 Berlin, Exhibition Rooms at Zoo

1910 Hanover, Hall of Arts and Crafts
Copenhagen, Zoo
Leipzig, House of German Bookprinting
Liegnitz, Art Club
Munich, Altes Rathaus
Posen, Kaiser-Friedrich-Museum

1911 Mannheim, City Art Gallery

1912 Bromberg, School of Arts and Crafts
Copenhagen, Lithographic Institution
Littau, Crafts Club
New York, Salmagundi Club
Tiflis
Vienna, *Secession*
Vienna, Austrian Museum of Art and Industry
Zurich, Helmhaus

1913 Bremen, Art Gallery
Breslau, (Union of Bookprinters)
Düsseldorf, Museum of Arts and Crafts
Frankfurt am Main, Festival Hall
Geneva
Hagen, Folkwang Museum
Leipzig, P. H. Beyer & Son
Travelling Exhibition (Association of the German Typographic Company, Leipzig)

1914 Bonn, Obernier Museum
Cologne, (Society for the Promotion of the Creative Arts)
Leipzig, Hall of Industry
London, Doré Gallery
Mannheim, Art Gallery
Munich, Theresienhöhe Exhibition Park
New York, National Arts Club
Rochester, Memorial Art Gallery
Rotterdam, Gebouw de Doele

BIBLIOGRAPHY

Friedrich Ahlers-Hestermann, Stilwende — Aufbruch der Jugend um 1900, Berlin 1941
Jacques Albachary (Ed.), Plakat Handbuch Albacharys Führer durch das Plakatwesen, Berlin Ausgabe 1928
Hans Ankwicz von Kleehoven, Josef Hoffmann, in: Große Österreicher, Vol. 10, Zürich, Leipzig and Vienna 1957, pp. 171—179
Hans Ankwicz von Kleehoven, Felician Freiherr von Myrbach-Rheinfeld, in: Große Österreicher, Vol. 13, Zurich, Leipzig and Vienna 1959, pp. 137—145
Hans Ankwicz von Kleehoven, Die Anfänge der Wiener Secession, in: Alte und moderne Kunst, Vol. 5, June/July 1960, pp. 6—10
Hans Ankwicz von Kleehoven, Die Wiener Werkstätte, in: Alte und moderne Kunst, Vol. 12, 1967, No. 92, pp. 20—27
George Ashdown Audsley, The ornamental Arts of Japan, 3 Vols., London 1882
Hermann Bahr, Secession, Vienna 1900
Hermann Bahr, Rede über Klimt, Vienna 1901
Hermann Bahr, Gegen Klimt, Vienna 1903
Richard Bamberger and Franz Maier-Bruck (Ed.), Österreich Lexikon, 2 Vols., Vienna and Munich 1966
M. Bauwens, T. Hayashi u. a., Les Affiches Étrangères illustrées, Paris 1897
Ilse Breiner-Neckel, Das Plakat der Wiener Secession, unpublished dissertation, Vienna 1958
Justus Brinckmann, Japanische Flächenornamente, Aarau 1892
Walter Crane, The Basis of Design, London 1898
Walter Crane, Line and Form, London 1900
Walter Crane, Ideals in Art, London 1905
Rudolf Cronau, Das Buck der Reklame, Leipzig 1889
Thomas W. Cutler, A Grammar of Japanese Ornament and Design, London 1880
Freidrich Deneken, Japanische Motive für Flächenverzierung, Berlin 1897
Josef Engelhart, Ein Wiener Maler erzählt, Vienna 1943
Rupert Feuchtmüller und Wilhelm Mrazek, Kunst in Österreich 1860—1918, Vienna 1964
Günther Feuerstein, Wiener Bauten 1900 bis heute, published by Karl Schwanzer, Vienna 1964
Justinian Frisch, Das Wiener Straßenbild, Vienna 1928 (=Die Straßenreklame der Weltstädte I.)
Monika Fritz, Der Wiener Maler Carl Moll, unpublished dissertation, Innsbruck 1962
Eugène Grasset, La plante et ses applications ornementales, Paris n.d. (1896)
Eugène Grasset, Méthode de composition ornementale, 2 Vols., Paris, n.d. (1905)
Ernst Growald, Der Plakat-Spiegel Erfahrungssätze für Plakat-Künstler und Besteller, Berlin, n.d.
G. H. E. Hawkins, Poster Advertising, Chicago 1910
D. C. A. Hémet, Traité pratique de Publicité Commerciale et Industrielle, Paris 1912
Friedrich Hesse, Die Chromolithographie, Halle a. S. 1906
Ludwig Hevesi, Acht Jahre Secession 1897—1905, Vienna 1906
Ludwig Hevesi, Hugo Haberfeld und A. S. Levetus, The Art-Revival in Austria, The Studio, Special Summer Number 1906
Ludwig Hevisi, Altkunst — Neukunst, Wien 1894—1908, Vienna 1909
Charles Hiatt, Picture Posters, London 1895
Josef Hoffmann, Koloman Moser, Fritz Waerndorfer, WW Wiener Werkstaette, Productiv-Genossenschaft von Kunsthandwerkern in Wien, Vienna 1905
Werner Hofmann, Moderne Malerei in Österreich, Vienna 1965
Karel Holešovský, 100 Plakátů z přelomu století, Exhibition Catalogue Brno 1966 (Moravská galerie v Brně)
Karel Holešovský, Sezessionistische Plakatkunst in Böhmen, in: Alte und moderne Kunst, Vol. 12, 1967, No. 94, pp. 29—35
Owen Jones, The Grammar of Ornament, London 1856
Otto Kamm, Datierungsfragen bei Kokoschka, in: Alte und moderne Kunst, Vol. 6, 1961, No. 42, p. 28
Julius Klinger, Hagen und Dortmund 1912 (=Monographien deutscher Reklamekünstler, No. III.)
Robert Koch, The Poster Movement and Art Nouveau, in: Gazette des Beaux-Arts, Vol. 50, 1957, pp. 285—296
Judith Koós, Dies Auswirkungen des Jugendstils in Ungarn, in: Alte und moderne Kunst, Vol. 14, 1969, No. 102, pp. 23—31
Herm. Cl. Kosel (Ed.), Deutsch-österreichisches Künstler- und Schriftsteller-Lexikon, 2 Vols., Vienna 1902
Horst-Herbert Kossatz, Unbekannte Wiener Reklame-Plakate, in: Alte und moderne Kunst, Vol. 13 1968, No. 100, 28—35
Horst-Herbert Kossatz, Plakate des Jugendstils im Österreichischen Museum für angewandte Kunst, in: Alte und moderne Kunst, Vol. 14 1969, No. 102, p. 53
Horst-Herbert Kossatz, Die graphischen Künste und die Photographie — Ein Beitrag zum Verständnis des 19. Jahrhunderts, in: Alte und moderne Kunst, Vol. 14, 1969, No. 104, pp. 15—24
Horst-Herbert Kossatz, Neuentdeckte Plakate, in: Albertina-Informationen 3, 1969, pp. 4—6
Helene Kowalski, Die Stellung der Wiener Werkstätte in der Entwicklung des Kunstgewerbes seit 1900, unpublished dissertation, Vienna 1951
Otto F. W. Krüger, Die Illustrationsverfahren, Leipzig 1914
Clay Lancaster, Oriental Contributions to Art Nouveau, in: The Art Bulletin, Vol. 34, 1952, pp. 297—310
Rudolf von Larisch, Über Leserlichkeit von ornamentalen Schriften, Vienna 1904
Rudolf von Larisch, Unterricht in ornamentaler Schrift, Vienna 1905
Joseph Aug. Lux, Das neue Kunstgewerbe in Deutschland, Leipzig 1908
Stephan Tschudi Madsen, Sources of Art Nouveau, Oslo 1956
Ernest Maindron, Les Affiches illustrées, Paris 1886
Ernest Maindron, Les Affiches illustrées (1886—1895), Paris 1896
Ottokar Mascha, Österreichische Plakatkunst, Vienna, n.d. (1915)
Victor Mataja, Die Reklame, Leipzig 1910
J. Matthias, Die Formensprache des Kunstgewerbes, Liegnitz 1875
Anton Mayer, Wiens Buchdrucker-Geschichte, Vol. 2, Vienna 1887
Max Mell, Alfred Roller, Vienna and Leipzig 1922 (=Die Wiedergabe, 1. Reihe, 2 vols)
D. H. Moser, Book of Japanese Ornamentation, composing Designs for the use of Signpainters, Decorators, Designers, Silversmiths, and many other purposes, London 1880
Wilhelm Mrazek, Die Wiener Werkstätte, Modernes Kunsthandwerk von 1903—1932, Vienna 1966 (Kulturnachrichten aus Osterreich)
Christian M. Nebehay, Catalogue 92, Die Wiener Werkstätte und die Kunst um 1900, Vienna 1965
Christian M. Nebehay, Catalogue 96, Graphik um 1900, Vienna, n.d. (1967)
Christian M. Nebehay, Gustav Klimt Dokumentation, Vienna 1969
Walther Maria Neuwirth, Die sieben heroischen Jahre der Wiener Moderne, in: Alte und moderne Kunst, Vol. 9., 1964, No. 74, pp. 28—31
Fritz Novotny und Johannes Dobai, Gustav Klimt, Salzburg 1967
Erwin Paneth, Entwicklung der Reklame von Altertum bis zur Gegenwart, Munich and Berlin 1926
Martin Paul, Technischer Führer durch Wien, Vienna 1910
Edward Penfield (Introduction), Posters in Miniature, London and New York 1896
Vittorio Pica, Attraverso gli Albi e le Cartelle, Bergamo 1902
M. A. Racinet, L'Ornement polychrome, Paris 1869—1873
Hellmut Rademacher, Das deutsche Plakat, Dresden 1965
Leopold Reidemeister, Der Japonismus in der Malerei und Graphik des 19. Jahrhunderts, Exhibition Catalogue, Staatliche Museen Preußischer Kulturbesitz, Berlin 1965
W. S. Rogers, A Book of the Poster, London 1901
J. V. Scheybal, Katalog uměleckých plakatů z obdobi 1890—1915, Liberec 1966
Fritz Schmalenbach, Ein Beitrag zu Theorie und Geschichte der Flächenkunst, Würzburg 1935
Rudolf Schmidt, Das Wiener Künstlerhaus, Eine Chronik 1861—1951, Vienna 1951
Hans Sachs, Schriften über Reklamekunst, Berlin-Charlottenburg 1920 (=Handbücher der Reklamekunst III.)
Anton Sailer, Das Plakat, Munich 1965
Eduard F. Sekler, The Stoclet House by Josef Hoffmann, in: Essays in The History of

Architecture, presented to Rudolf Wittkower, London 1967, pp. 228—244
Helmut Seling (Ed.) and Kurt Bauch (Preface), Jugendstil — Der Weg ins 20. Jahrhundert, Heidelberg and Munich 1959
Gottfried Semper, Der Stil in den technischen und tektonischen Künsten oder Praktische Ästhetik, 2 Vols., Frankfurt a. M. 1860 and 1863
Richard Sommer, Graphik, Druck und Reproduktion, Vienna 1927

EXHIBITION CATALOGUES

Catalogue d'Affiches Illustrées Anciennes et Modernes (Librairie Ed. Sogot) Paris 1891
Austellung Künstlerischer Plakate, Dresden 1896
Katalog der Ausstellung deutscher Plakate, Aachen 1897
Austellungskataloge der Vereinigung bildender Künstler Österreichs Secession, Vienna 1898—1914
Austellungskataloge des Hagenbundes, Vienna 1900—1914
Kunstschau Wien 1908, Vienna 1908
Internationale Kunstschau Wien 1909, Vienna 1909
Frühjahrsausstellung, Österr. Kunstgewerbe verbunden mit einer Austellung der k. k. Kunstgewerbeschule, Vienna 1912
Das Plakat als Kunstwerk (Hagenbund), Vienna 1934 (typed manuscript)
Plakate um 1900, Darmstadt 1962
Plakat- und Buchkunst um 1900, Hamburg 1963
Wien um 1900, Vienna 1964
Secession Europäische Kunst um die Jahrhundertwende, Munich 1964
Europäischer Jugendstil, Bremen 1965
Jugendstil & Expressionism in German Posters, Berkeley 1965/66
Česká secese umění 1900, Brno 1966
Die Wiener Werkstätte, Vienna 1967
Koloman Moser 1868—1918, Graz 1969
Charles Rennie Mackintosh, Vienna 1969
Österreichische Aktzeichnungen von Klimt bis heute, Vienna 1969
Jugendstil — Wiener Secession, Kunsterhaus Palais Thurn und Taxis 1971
Vienna Secession: Art Nouveau to 1970, Royal Academy, London 1971
Kristian Sotriffer, Malerei und Plastik in Österreich, Von Makart bis Wotruba, Vienna and Munich 1963
Jean Louis Sponsel, Das Moderne Plakat, Dresden 1897
Alice Strobl, Zu den Fakultätsbildern von Gustav Klimt, in: Albertina-Studien, No. 4 1964, pp. 138—169
W. Tuer, Das Buch reizender und merkwürdiger Zeichnungen, Leipzig 1894
F. Rudolf Uebe, Die Sammlung angewandter Graphik, Verzeichnis der sammelnden Mitglieder des Vereins der Plakatfreunde E. V., Berlin-Charlottenburg 1919 (=Handbücher der Reklamekunst I.)
F. Rudolf Uebe, Künstlerzeichen — Zusammenstellung von 456 Zeichen deutscher und ausländischer Reklamekünstler, Berlin-Charlottenburg 1919 (=Handbücher der Reklamekunst II.)
Arthur W. Unger, Die Herstellung von Büchern, Illustrationen, Akzidenzen etc., Halle a S. 1923
Heinrich Waentig, Wirtschaft und Kunst, Jena 1909
Paul Wember, Die Jugend der Plakate 1887—1917, Krefeld, n.d.
Hans Maria Wingler, Oskar Kokoschka Schriften 1907—1955, Munich 1956
Berta Zuckerkandl, Zeitkunst, Wien 1901—1907, Vienna and Leipzig 1908
Berta Zuckerkandl-Szeps, Ich erlebte 50 Jahre Weltgeschichte, Stockholm 1935
Walter von Zur Westen, Reklamekunst, Bielefeld and Leipzig 1903 (=Sammlung Illustrierter Monographien Vol. 13)

PERIODICALS

Mittheilungen des k. k. Österr. Museums für Kunst und Industrie, Vienna 1865 to 1897
Jahresberichte des k. k. Österr. Museums für Kunst und Industrie, Vienna
L'Estampe et L'Affiche, Paris 1897—1899
Ver Sacrum, Vienna 1898, Leipzig 1899, Vienna 1900—1903
Kunst und Kunsthandwerk, Vienna 1898—1921
La Plume, Album trimestriel illustré des Affiches & Estampes, Paris 1898—1900
Propaganda, Berlin 1898—1900
The Poster, London 1898—1900
Das Interieur, Vienna 1900—1914
Moderne Reklame, Berlin 1902—1904
Das Andere, Vienna 1903
Der liebe Augustin, Vienna 1904
Hohe Warte, Vienna 1904—1908
Die Fläche, Vienna 1902/3 and 1910
Das Plakat, Berlin 1910—1921
Jahrbuch des Deutschen Werkbundes 1913, Jena 1913 (=Die Kunst in Industrie und Handel)
Der Aufbau, Vol. 19. 1964, No. 4/5